JESUS INVITES US TO DIALOGUE WITH HIM—"I have called you friends because I have revealed to you everything that I have heard from my Father. You did not choose me. Rather, I chose you" (John 15:15-16).

INSPIRATIONAL THOU
FOR EVERY DAY

INSPIRATIONAL THOUGHTS
FOR EVERY DAY

MINUTE MEDITATIONS FOR EVERY DAY
CONTAINING A SCRIPTURE READING,
A REFLECTION, AND A PRAYER

By
REV. THOMAS J. DONAGHY

Illustrated

CATHOLIC BOOK PUBLISHING CORP.
New Jersey

CONTENTS

In honor of the living and deceased members of Sigma Beta Kappa fraternity, La Salle College.

NIHIL OBSTAT: Rev. James M. Cafone, M.A., S.T.D.
Censor Librorum

IMPRIMATUR: ✠ Most Rev. John J. Myers, D.D., J.C.D.
Archbishop of Newark

(T-194)

ISBN 978-1-937913-55-7

© 2004 Catholic Book Publishing Corp., N.J.
Printed in China
www.catholicbookpublishing.com

INTRODUCTION

SOME years ago, following a Nuptial Mass, my few personal words to the couple were, "No matter what happens, never stop talking with one another." Several years later, the couple, with all their children now in junior and senior high school, asked me if I remembered what I told them before they went down the aisle. There was no bluffing, because I did not remember.

They shared what I said, while, at the same time, noting that their determination to never stop communicating preserved their happy marriage through good times and bad.

Maintaining communication with everyone is a common-sense way to achieve a better quality of life. Ever more so is the case in our most important relationship, namely, our intimacy with God. Over the ages, this has been the thrust of Scripture, the Saints and spiritual writers. There are so many times throughout each day, as we go about our chosen role in life, when a free minute here, or a ten-minute break there provides an excellent opportunity to communicate with the Lord.

This work is presented as a support for speaking with God many times throughout the day. A word or sentence from the Scripture reading, reflection, or prayer may easily become a mantra for the day, one that enables us to follow St. Augustine's admonition, "Pray in season and out."

Father Thomas J. Donaghy

Prayer of Ardent Longing for God

O GOD,
  You are my God Whom I earnestly
    seek;
for You my flesh longs and my soul
    thirsts
as in a parched and weary land where
    there is no water.
Hence I have gazed toward You in the
    sanctuary
and have beheld Your power and Your
    glory.
Because Your love is better than life,
my lips will glorify You.

Thus I will bless You as long as I live;
lifting up my hands,
I will call upon Your Name.

THE Lord let His face shine upon you, and be gracious to you. The Lord look upon you with kindness and grant you peace. —Num 6:25-26

JAN.
1

REFLECTION. The world tells us that it is resolution time.

We may want to imitate the peace and light of Jesus and Mary as we prepare to go forward as another year begins.

PRAYER. *God, our Father, let us always walk in the light and peace of Your love and care for Your people. May we strive to follow in the footsteps of Jesus and Mary.*

THE Lord has made known His salvation; He has manifested His righteousness for all the nations to see. —Ps 98:2

JAN.
2

REFLECTION. In faith, we know that our salvation turns on the way that we treat one another.

As a fallen people, all we ask for is justice. It is justice that we must offer one another.

PRAYER. *Just Father, be with us in our daily lives. May we imitate Your mercy and justice in all things.*

Y lips will proclaim Your righteous deeds and Your salvation all day long. . . . —Ps 71:15

JAN. 3

REFLECTION. The salvation of the world has been brought about through the birth of a small Child.

Therefore, we come to understand the gentle God we call Father.

PRAYER. *Come to us, Lord, and spread Your peace and justice in our minds, hearts, homes and workplaces. May we be the instruments of Your love and peace.*

 ND I myself have seen and have testified that this is the Son of God. —Jn 1:34

JAN. 4

REFLECTION. Rejoicing in our Savior, we search out the ways to bring the Good News of our salvation to our family, friends and relatives.

Imitating the gentleness of Jesus is a good way to start.

PRAYER. *Lord Jesus, come to us as we rejoice in Your birth. Lead us along the path of generosity and goodness to one another.*

HAT grace has now been revealed by the appearance of our Savior Jesus Christ. He has abolished death and brought life and immortality to light through the Gospel. —2 Tim 1:10

JAN. 5

REFLECTION. Indeed, the grace of God has been revealed.

The reality that life will never end for those who seek God in all things has blossomed.

PRAYER. *God, our Father, our hearts are filled with joy and praise for the great gift of everlasting life. In our love for each other, may we always reflect Your love in our hearts. Enable us to walk hand in hand with our poor, nourished with Your grace and presence.*

 OR the Lord desires that a father be honored by his children, and He confirms the mother's rights over her children. —Sir 3:2

JAN. 6

REFLECTION. When we contemplate any family unit, the simple resolve of each member to accomplish God's Will in everyday life is a blessing.

It will be a great source of grace and holiness for that particular family.

PRAYER. *Almighty God, Father of all, we earnestly entreat You for Your care and concern for families throughout the world. In our love for one another, may we always live according to Your Word, fostering peace and joy among our brothers and sisters.*

9

HERE is the newborn King of the Jews? We saw the rising of His star, and we have come to pay Him homage. —Mt 2:2

JAN. 7

REFLECTION. The celebration of the opening of God's Word, and in particular the message of salvation, speaks volumes to us in our relationships with others.

How careful we must be to open our minds and hearts to all peoples.

PRAYER. *Lord, our God, like the kings of old, each day we seek the brilliance of the light of Christ. Bless us with all good that we might hasten our conversion of mind and heart so that we may live in the glow of the Messianic redemption.*

———————

 E replied, "Give them something to eat yourselves." They said to Him, "Are we to go and spend two hundred denarii on bread for them to eat?" —Mk 6:37

JAN. 8

REFLECTION. Jesus had compassion on the people who had been following Him and listening to Him.

We have at hand the Bread of Angels to nourish us as we strive to live His Word.

PRAYER. *God, our Father, be with us as we approach the holies of holies to be nourished by the Body and Blood of Christ. Make us as worthy as possible for this great Gift.*

HE mountains will yield peace for the people, and the hills, righteousness. —Ps 72:3

JAN. 9

REFLECTION. Today, we retreat to our private place to talk with God.

We know that wherever our holy mountain is, we will be bathed in peace and justice.

PRAYER. *Let us come to You with joy, O Lord, knowing that You will make all things right according to Your compassion and love.*

 AY His glorious Name be blessed forever, and may the whole world be filled with His glory. Amen. Amen. —Ps 72:19

JAN. 10

REFLECTION. As followers of Jesus, we walk in His Name. We are the glory of God on earth, reflecting God's great love for His people.

As a people of joy, we bring light to the world and into the lives of all.

PRAYER. *Almighty God, in Your great wisdom You sent Your Son, Jesus, to bring the light, peace, and joy of Your Kingdom to earth. Let us always rejoice in Your light with shouts of peace and joy.*

HE Spirit of the Lord is upon Me, because He has anointed Me to bring the Good News to the poor. —Lk 4:18

JAN. 11

REFLECTION. We measure our wealth by the closeness of our relationship with God.

Sin can separate us from the Lord, and the earthly presence of Jesus reminds us to abstain from sin.

PRAYER. *Loving Father, help Your people to walk always in the Spirit. May we choose the light of the Spirit over the darkness of evil.*

———————

 HEN Jesus saw him lying there and was aware that he had been ill for a long time, He said to him, "Do you want to get well?"

—Jn 5:6

JAN. 12

REFLECTION. Every day of our lives, Jesus constantly asks us if we want to be well.

The medicine of doing God's Will in our regard cures us of all that would keep us from the presence of God.

PRAYER. *Almighty Father, in Your kindness for us You sent Your Son to walk with us through the valley of darkness. Let us always follow the light of Jesus.*

, THE Lord, have called you to serve the cause of right; I have taken you by the hand and formed you; I have appointed you as covenant of the people and light of the nations. —Isa 42:6

JAN.
13

REFLECTION. As Light of the world, Jesus is entitled to all the glory and praise we can muster.

This Good News is healing balm for the world and our society. The news is so important that we must continue to bring the message of salvation to as many people as possible.

PRAYER. *Heavenly Father, You know the goodwill of Your people and their desire to serve You. May Your living grace and sacraments be ever available through the ministry of those whom You call to serve Your Church as priests.*

OW can I repay the Lord for all the good He has done for me?
—Ps 116:12

JAN.
14

REFLECTION. We strive each day to grasp the providence of God in all that He has given us and all that He will give us to the end.

Our care and development of our God-given gifts is all the praise and thanks the Lord desires.

PRAYER. *We rejoice in Your great goodness to us, O Lord. May we never forget You as we grow and expand the talents so freely given to us.*

THE time of fulfillment has arrived, and the Kingdom of God is close at hand. Repent, and believe in the Gospel.

JAN.
15

—Mk 1:15

REFLECTION. In the tasks of everyday life we are urged not to forget that the Kingdom of God is close by.

We endeavor to walk always in God's grace, so that, if called, we may slip into the vineyard effortlessly.

PRAYER. *We praise You, Lord God Almighty, in all our works and prayers each day. Let us never forget You and Your love for us.*

AMUEL told him everything and concealed nothing from him. Eli then said: "He is the Lord. He will do what seems best in His judgment."

JAN.
16

—1 Sam 3:18

REFLECTION. What a valuable lesson we have in God's Word.

Simply trusting in the Lord will enable us to accomplish all those things in life that God has in mind for us.

PRAYER. *Lord our God, we acknowledge Your universal presence. May we always remember that You are with us at all times and trust in Your care for us.*

E cured many who were afflicted with various diseases, and He drove out many demons, although He would not permit them to speak because they knew Who He was. **JAN. 17** —Mk 1:34

REFLECTION. Like the Israelites of old, we turn to Jesus so that He might cure us of our sinfulness.

May He drive away those demons that lead us into temptation.

PRAYER. *God, our Father, with great humility and simplicity we come to You so that we might be cured of our sins. May we have the courage to avoid occasions of sin.*

———

 MAN with leprosy approached and, kneeling before Him, begged him, "If You choose to do so, You can make me clean." **JAN. 18** —Mk 1:40

REFLECTION. We please the Lord Jesus when we acknowledge our need for His help.

He stands willing and ready to be of service in making us closer to Him and the Father.

PRAYER. *O Lord, our God, You are always ready to receive us when we need Your help. Help us to turn to You and away from temptation.*

BLESSED are the people who know how to acclaim You, O Lord, who walk in the light of Your countenance.

JAN.
19

—Ps 89:16

REFLECTION. We have much to be joyful and shout about. The Lord our God has come to redeem us, taking the form of a little Child.

We live in the light of His innocence.

PRAYER. *Heavenly Father, Your children praise You for the gift of everlasting life. May our childlike simplicity win for us the reward of eternal light.*

I AM honored in the sight of the Lord. My God is now my strength.

JAN.
20

—Isa 49:5

REFLECTION. Jesus, the Light of the nations, came to do the Will of the Father.

We share that light through our baptism, as well as the responsibility to carry the light for the Lord Who has returned to the Father.

PRAYER. *God, our Father, let us walk always in the light of Your Divine Son. Help us to be light for one another and for the world.*

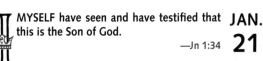 MYSELF have seen and have testified that this is the Son of God.

—Jn 1:34

REFLECTION. The deep faith of John the Baptist is a model for modern Christians who walk in the midst of a firestorm of criticism, questioning, and sometimes bigotry.

Like John we stand firm in the midst of opposition, holding fast to our belief in the Redeemer Son of God.

PRAYER. *Lord, we cry out to You to protect us from the forces of evil that would dissuade us from Your Divine truth. May we live and speak the Faith, trusting in Your generous protection.*

 OES the Lord take as much delight in burnt offerings and sacrifices as in obedience to the voice of the Lord? Surely obedience is better than sacrifice, and submissiveness is better than the fat of rams. —1 Sam 15:22

REFLECTION. When we generously accept God's Word, especially in the Commandments, we are doing God's Will in all things.

To live the Will of God is the greatest sacrifice and personal denial.

PRAYER. *Almighty God, we see in Your Son perfect conformity to Your Will. May we always seek to do what You command in a generous and joyful way.*

UT the time will come when the Bridegroom is taken away from them, and
then on that day they will fast.

JAN.
23

—Mk 2:20

REFLECTION. Jesus, our Bridegroom, has been
taken from us in one sense. But He remains
with us through His Sacraments and His
Word.

We fast from sin in anticipation of His return to take us with Him to the Father.

PRAYER. *Almighty God, watch over Your peo-*
ple as they strive to remain faithful to Jesus.
Keep us free from any kind of sensuality that
would make the Lord ashamed of us.

 WILL sing a new song to You, my God; on
a ten-stringed lyre I will play music for
You.

JAN.
24

—Ps 144:9

REFLECTION. In joyful praise we raise our
minds, hearts, and voices in thanksgiving to
God for giving us this day with all of its possi-
bilities to do good.

We joyfully look forward to joining the
heavenly choirs after a life of grace and
virtue.

PRAYER. *O Lord, our God, we raise our minds*
and hearts to You in grateful praise for having
given us life. Keep us in Your love and grace
that we might live with You forever.

THEY watched Him closely to see whether He would cure him on the Sabbath so that they might accuse Him. —Mk 3:2

JAN. 25

REFLECTION. The subtle persecution of Jesus can easily be reflected in our own experiences of those who judge us unjustly.

What a badge of honor for Christ's followers to be rashly judged because of our faith in love, life, and peace.

PRAYER. *O most gracious God, in our faith lives we encounter the arrows of false judgment and exclusion. Help us to live patiently with these encounters in imitation of Jesus.*

HE had healed so many that all who were afflicted in any way came crowding around to touch Him. —Mk 3:10

JAN. 26

REFLECTION. As we press on through the winter of cold and flu, our faith tells us that should we contract the disease of sin, we can be readily cured by turning to the Lord in deep sorrow.

He wants and waits to heal us.

PRAYER. *God, our loving Father, through the merits of Your Divine Son, Jesus, we rejoice in the assurance that our sins can be forgiven. Grant us the grace every day to practice perfect contrition.*

19

HEN Paul replied, "What are you doing, weeping and breaking my heart? For I am ready not only to be bound but even to die in Jerusalem for the Name of the Lord Jesus."

JAN. 27

—Acts 21:13

REFLECTION. As sons and daughters of the Lord, like Paul, we live and die for the Lord.

We constantly struggle in the Name of the Lord to walk always in the light and thus, when called, to die in the Lord.

PRAYER. *We praise You, heavenly Father, for giving us Your servant Paul as a source of inspiration and good example. May we, like Paul, willingly fight the wiles of the evil one to the end.*

———————

 Y foes pursue me all day long, with their forces too many to number. When I am terrified, I place my trust in You.

JAN. 28

—Ps 56:3-4

REFLECTION. Today we live in a largely changed life mode. Conscious of possible sudden death and destruction, natural fears surface and tempt us to freeze.

With deep and abiding trust in God, we lead our normal lives, remaining calm and in prayer.

PRAYER. *O Lord, our God, show Your goodness to Your people and protect us from sudden and unprovided death. Grant us the wisdom to trust only in You through lives of virtue and peace.*

I AM grateful to God—Whom I worship with a clean conscience as did my ancestors—when I remember you constantly in my prayers night and day. —2 Tim 1:3

JAN.
29

REFLECTION. The early Christians had a great love for one another.

Their prayerful bonds helped them to combat fierce struggles with those who wished to destroy their faith-filled love for one another.

PRAYER. *In the midst of great turmoil in our world, we cry to You, loving Father. Help us to love one another and seek to serve the interests of all our worshiping communities.*

———————

 HE said to them: "The harvest is abundant, but the laborers are few. Therefore, ask the Lord of the harvest to send forth laborers for His harvest."
—Lk 10:2

JAN.
30

REFLECTION. As followers of Christ, our universal call to holiness is, at the same time, a message to seek folks from every facet of life to work for and with God's people.

Depending on time and circumstance, we encourage individuals to become servants of the Lord and harvest workers.

PRAYER. *Lord, our God, we seek Your generosity in granting the gift of reaping Your harvest. Turning away from home and hearth to work in the vineyard can be challenging. Help us not to falter.*

RETHREN, I exhort you in the Name of our Lord Jesus Christ to be in full agreement with one another and not permit divisions to arise among you. Be perfectly united in mind and purpose.

—1 Cor 1:10

REFLECTION. It is inevitable that the barque of Peter will encounter rough sailing. This is why we must stand together in faith and doctrine.

Sometimes our morning prayer could easily include the Apostles' Creed as a reminder of our beliefs.

PRAYER. *God, our Father, Your Son, our Lord, Jesus Christ, exhorts us to be one in mind and heart with Pope and Church. May we always listen attentively to our Holy Father and Your Word.*

_____

AVE mercy on me, O God, in accord with Your kindness; in Your abundant compassion wipe away my offenses.

—Ps 51:3

REFLECTION. Who among us does not need the Lord's mercy?

We are singularly blessed in the knowledge of God's great love for us, knowing that at any time and in every circumstance, we will receive mercy simply by asking.

PRAYER. *God, our Father, as a pilgrim Church we seek Your mercy. In times of temptation and sin, grant us the grace to turn to You with hope for Your mercy and love.*

WHO will endure the day of His coming, and who can stand when He appears? For He is like the refiner's fire, or like the fuller's soap. —Mal 3:2

FEB. 2

REFLECTION. When Jesus was presented in the temple, He really was coming home and into His own. Not only would He be the Light of the world, but also He would judge the nations.

How blessed we are to have Jesus as Judge.

PRAYER. *Lord, our God, we come to You with praise and thanksgiving. Make us live our lives so that Jesus, our Judge, will be pleased with His people.*

I WILL leave in your midst a people humble and lowly as a remnant. They shall seek refuge in the Name of the Lord. —Zep 3:12

FEB. 3

REFLECTION. Expelling our self-pride, we walk in the way of the Lord, counting our blessings and living in peace with others, especially those in our family.

We are indeed called to be God's holy remnant.

PRAYER. *Lord of heaven and earth, we pray for humility and simplicity in our daily lives. Help us to bring Your goodness and Your mercy to others.*

PERHAPS the Lord will look upon my misery and will repay me for the curses he is uttering today. —2 Sam 16:12

REFLECTION. Shimei was cursing David as David approached Bahurim with his army. Without invoking his kingly stature and status, David accepted this personal insult and left it to God to settle.

How often we are better off leaving disputes to the Lord and His Will.

PRAYER. *God, our Father, Your chosen servant David allowed patience to prevail in the midst of insults. He trusted You to be with him in a moment of degradation. Let us practice this patience in our lives.*

 HAVING heard about Jesus, she came up behind Him in the crowd and touched His cloak, for she thought, "If I simply touch His clothing, I shall be made well." —Mk 5: 27-28

REFLECTION. As we pass through the challenges of winter, our faith may begin to turn cold.

Like the woman with the flow of blood, we seek to move closer to Jesus and allow ourselves to be touched by His loving warmth.

PRAYER. *Jesus, Son of the living God, we come to You in faith. Help us to remain close to You so that we might walk in Your light and presence.*

IFT up your arches, O gates; rise up, you ancient portals, so that the King of glory may come in. **FEB. 6** —Ps 24:7

REFLECTION. We open ourselves, minds and hearts, spirits and emotions, to all that Jesus has taught us by His preaching and actions.

We take advantage of every avenue of intimacy with the Lord spoken in Scripture. We want to get closer and closer to the Lord, our God.

PRAYER. *In union with the Saints, we beg You O Lord, to come to us at every moment. Keep us free from the illusions of worldly success, and make us ever mindful of the poor.*

BSERVE the mandate of the Lord, your God. Follow His ways and observe His statutes, commands, ordinances, and decrees as written in the Law of Moses, that you may be successful in whatever you do, wherever you turn. **FEB. 7** —1 Ki 2:3

REFLECTION. The Commandments of God are the antithesis of "success" as understood in the world.

We recall in our personal lives how the observance of the Commandments has saved us from great harm.

PRAYER. *Draw near to us, O Lord, and keep us in Your care. May the Commandments be for us a crown of glory.*

N everything he did he offered thanks to the Holy One, proclaiming the glory of the Most High. He sang hymns of praise with all his heart to demonstrate his love for his Maker. —Sir 47:8

FEB.
8

REFLECTION. Like David, we have to remind ourselves each day of the great blessings God has bestowed upon us.

The way in which we live out God's Will according to His Word and Commandments is our lived praise.

PRAYER. *We praise You, Lord God Almighty, for the wonders of Your love for us and Your great gift of everlasting life.*

 E said to them, "Come away with Me, by yourselves, to a deserted place and rest for a while." For people continued to come and go in great numbers, and they had no time even to eat. —Mk 6:31

FEB.
9

REFLECTION. We have a standing invitation to go and be with the Lord in the silence of a special place.

We consciously make that place wherever we choose and know that we can be there both silent and alone except for Christ.

PRAYER. *God, our Father, give us the grace to be built up in our lives by Your silent presence. May we come to You with open minds and hearts to drink in Your being with us.*

IF anyone has caused distress, he has done so not only to me but to some extent—not to exaggerate—to all of you. —2 Cor 2:5

FEB. 10

REFLECTION. Paul reminds the Church of Corinth that divisiveness in the worshiping community can be harmful to the entire group. When we sin individually, we harm the entire fabric of society.

We nurse our hurts in love, not revenge.

PRAYER. *Father Almighty, be patient with us as we fail from time to time to live Your Word. Make us aware of our responsibility to the community to lead a life of virtue.*

WE heard of it in Ephrathah; we came upon it in the fields of Jaar. Let us enter His dwelling place, let us worship at His footstool. —Ps 132:6-7

FEB. 11

REFLECTION. The blessings of God are available to the entire world. By our personal lives of goodness, we are living testimony to the truth of God's universal love for all people.

We rejoice and take heart in His love.

PRAYER. *God of the universe, let Your light go before us so that we may always walk in Your ways and dwell forever in Your temple.*

YOU thrust aside the Commandment of God in order to preserve the traditions of men. —Mk 7:8

FEB.
12

REFLECTION. We enjoy the freedom of the sons and daughters of God.

So we must be careful not to build up human traditions and customs that violate both the spirit and the letter of God's Law.

PRAYER. *Almighty God, King of heaven and earth, may we always take Your commands seriously. We ask that You enable us to avoid human laws and traditions that violate Your will.*

LORD, You have examined me and You know me. You know when I sit and when I stand; You perceive my thoughts from a distance.—Ps 139:1-2

FEB.
13

REFLECTION. The Psalmist rejoices in the all-embracing God. How wonderful is our God Who cares for our inmost thoughts.

What a blessing to walk always in the presence of God.

PRAYER. *Mary, you were privileged to live in your Son's presence in a very special way. Help us to realize how blessed we are to have Him with us at all times.*

28

HERE will be only a few left of you who were as many as the stars in heaven because you would not obey the voice of the Lord, your God.

FEB.
14

—Deut 28:62

REFLECTION. When we listen to the voice of God, we shall keep out of harm's way.

Listening to God through prayer, Scripture, and preaching can keep us safe forever, and nothing of this world can touch us.

PRAYER. *O Lord, our God, be with us as we make our way to You. May the Holy Spirit watch over us and fill us with respect for Your Word.*

———————

 Y fruit is better than gold, even the finest gold, and My return better than choice silver. —Prov 8:19

FEB.
15

REFLECTION. In God's eyes, His people are the ultimate wealth of creation. Once confirmed in good, we are the outcomes of God's Wisdom.

We will be the new silver and gold, higher than all creation.

PRAYER. *Almighty God, our Father, You call us to the unspeakable joys of heaven, abiding in Your presence forever. May we always overcome our weaknesses while keeping our eye steadfastly on the goal.*

UCH hope will not be doomed to disappointment, because the love of God has been poured into our hearts through the Holy Spirit that has been given to us.

FEB. 16

—Rom 5:5

REFLECTION. It would be wise for us to allow the great gift of the Holy Spirit to permeate our lives every day.

To live as a people of hope bespeaks a wellness not ordinarily found in the world.

PRAYER. *God, our Father, Your Son, Jesus, promised us the Holy Spirit. Help us to open our hearts to the Spirit's wisdom so that we may serve You better.*

 N the power of his spirit he saw the end of times, and he comforted the mourners in Zion. He revealed the future to the end of the ages and hidden things long before they occurred.

FEB. 17

—Sir 48:24-25

REFLECTION. The long-range view of the prophets inspired God's people to persevere in good.

We have seen the prophet fulfilled in the Person of Jesus. For us the future is now, and now is the time to take it seriously.

PRAYER. *Merciful Lord, as we make our way toward life everlasting, may we always take great care in following Your Word and Will in our lives.*

ALTHOUGH we had suffered and been shamefully mistreated at Philippi, as you surely recall, God gave us courage to declare the Gospel of God to you despite great opposition. —1 Thes 2:2

FEB.
18

REFLECTION. The great evangelizers in the early Church, through their writings and exhortations, have preserved for us God's precious message for His people.

The sufferings of the preachers and teachers have borne much fruit. All the more reason to learn and live the Word of God.

PRAYER. *Lord, our God, many of Your servants suffered great deprivations and scourgings to spread Your Word and prepare for us a wonderful heritage. May we always respond to Your heavenly guidance with courage and perseverance.* _____

AT this, Jesus turned and, looking at His disciples, rebuked Peter and said, "Get behind Me, Satan! You are thinking not as God does, but as men do." —Mk 8:33

FEB.
19

REFLECTION. When we are living in the world, we can easily take on the mindset of a secular society.

It is important for us to cultivate in our lives, with great care, God's way of looking at things and life in general. His Word guides us.

PRAYER. *Gracious God, You have prepared an everlasting banquet for us. Grant that we may not give into the siren calls of the world.*

EFORE the mountains were brought forth or the earth and the world came into existence, from everlasting to everlasting You are God. —Ps 90:2

FEB. 20

REFLECTION. The timelessness of our God excites our interest in the Creator.

We know that one day, as long as we strive to do God's Will, He will call us through the veil of time into His everlasting presence.

PRAYER. *Lord, our God, with the Psalmist, we sing of our longing to be with You forever. May we always strive in our personal lives to accomplish our eternal salvation.*

 Y the sweat of your face you shall eat bread, until you return to the ground from which you were taken. For you are dust, and to dust you shall return.

FEB. 21

—Gen 3:19

REFLECTION. Our long winter nights remind us of the approaching season of penance and conversion.

Remembering that we are dirt and that we shall all return to dirt is something to think about when we measure our lives in the sight of God.

PRAYER. *Lord God, You made us from the slime of the earth to which we will all one day return. Grant us the wisdom to repent of our sins and be converted to Your ways.*

REATE in me a clean heart, O God, ... Restore to me the joy of being saved. —Ps 51:12-14

FEB. 22

REFLECTION. When we consider the glories of God's creation, and all that goes into our human makeup, how sad that we sometimes clutter our minds and hearts with the tawdry.

Our salvation lies in purity of heart.

PRAYER. *Merciful Father, we have a tendency to corrupt the beauty of Your creation, especially in our minds and bodies. Grant us the discipline to avoid sins of the flesh.*

 F only you would listen to His voice today: "Harden not your hearts." —Ps 95:7-8

FEB. 23

REFLECTION. God speaks to us in many ways. At Mass we listen to Scripture and preaching.

Let us resolve during times of penance to take the Word of God seriously. Allow it to change our lives for the better.

PRAYER. *Loving Father, You instruct us in the ways of faith. Let Your Angels guide us along the right path, keeping us free from the wiles and snares of the devil.*

WAIT for the Lord in anxious expectation; I place my hope in His Word. . . . For with the Lord there is kindness, as well as plenteous redemption. —Ps 130:5-7

FEB. 24

REFLECTION. Our God is a God of mercy and trust.

In times of temptation we turn to Him with the assurance of grace and help. Convicted of sin, we return to Him, knowing that we will be forgiven.

PRAYER. *Merciful Lord, hear our cry for mercy as we return to You, repenting for our sins. May Your grace keep us from temptation and sin forever.*

 ID yourself of all your sins; and make a new heart and a new spirit. —Ezek 18:31

FEB. 25

REFLECTION. Here we find profound sociology. What would our world be like if we were able to rid ourselves of sin?

Renewed in mind and spirit, we can easily imagine a great age of peace, prosperity, and love.

PRAYER. *Lord, our God, we turn to You with hearts full of sorrow for our sins. Give us a glimpse of eternal life without sin by our living Your Commandments completely.*

DO not wish the sinner to die, says the Lord, but to turn to Me and live.

—Ezek 33:11

FEB. 26

REFLECTION. Our most generous and loving Father tells us of His great love for us. He wishes no harm to come to us.

Yet, only we, through cooperation with His graces, can walk through life without sin. This is what our Lord truly wants for us.

PRAYER. *Holy God, the generosity of love for Your people fills us with hope as we come to the realization of how destructive our sins can be. Help us to lift ourselves up from indifference and neglect in our response to Your love.*

 ITH all your heart turn to Me for I am tender and compassionate.

—Jl 2:12-13

FEB. 27

REFLECTION. What great peace enters our lives as we come to know the tender and compassionate God we have.

Our understanding should urge us on to greater determination to rid ourselves of sin and be converted.

PRAYER. *Almighty God, as we come closer to You in our time of penance and conversion, shower upon Your people the gifts of compassion and tenderness, so that we may be more like You in prayer and action.*

EEK good and not evil so that you may live, and the Lord will be with you.
—Am 5:14

FEB. 28

REFLECTION. Frequently, when we attend Mass, we hear the greeting, "The Lord be with you." When we join others in praising and worshiping God, we are indeed seeking good, asking for help to avoid evil.

So, even outside Mass, we should wish each other, "The Lord be with you." It can readily diffuse tense situations.

PRAYER. *Lord God, we have been assured that as long as we seek the good in Your creation You will be with us. May we always think and act toward others with their good in mind.*

 EPENT, for the Kingdom of Heaven is close at hand.
—Mt 4:17

MAR. 1

REFLECTION. One of our sure guides along the path of life is that we do not know when earthly life will come to an end.

How important that our repentance for past and present transgressions be a daily practice.

PRAYER. *Lord, our God, we do not know the length of our days. Help us to seek forgiveness every day You give us so that we may live assured of the Kingdom.*

BUT that which is on rich soil are the ones who, when they have heard the Word with a good and upright heart, keep it and yield a harvest through their perseverance. —Lk 8:15

REFLECTION. The discipline of our Lenten resolutions may seem very worthwhile when viewed in light of the goal.

This is true not only at the end of Lent, but also at the final moment of our lives.

PRAYER. *Heavenly Father, with generous spirits we have begun our Lenten conversion with good resolutions. May we persevere in good till the very end.*

I WILL depart from this place and go to my father, and I will say to him, "Father, I have sinned against heaven and against you." —Lk 15:18

REFLECTION. What a wonderful blessing we have in the Sacrament of Reconciliation.

With contrition we bring our sins to the Lord, and instantly we are forgiven and our misdeeds forgotten, never again to be held over us.

PRAYER. *Loving Father, You invite us to confession, contrition, and forgiveness. Help us to never put off confessing our sins that we might bask in the exhilaration of Your love.*

GOD so loved the world that He gave His only Son, so that everyone who believes in Him may not perish but may attain eternal life. —Jn 3:16

REFLECTION. As we meet the daily challenge of our Lenten choices, we are heartened by God's generosity in our regard.

What can we hold back from the Lord when we consider His having given us His Son?

PRAYER. *Merciful God, You give Your people so much that we are moved to return all that we can humanly accomplish. May we come to the realization of Your great love for us and return Your love as much as possible.*

———————

YOU have the words of eternal life. —Jn 6:68

REFLECTION. Sometimes, the noise and clamor of the world's ways nearly obscure the Word of God in our hearts.

Prayerful minutes throughout the day can save our minds and hearts for the Lord.

PRAYER. *Gracious God, rescue us from the mindless pursuits of the world. Through short whispered or reflective prayers, may we seek You in all things.*

AM the light of the world. The one who follows Me will never walk in darkness. Rather, he will have the light of life.

MAR.

6

—Jn 8:12

REFLECTION. Each day as we walk in the light of Christ, temptations of the wiley one are seen for what they are.

Both a sham and a pretense, evil suggestions can lead only to darkness.

PRAYER. *God, our Father, in Your great love for us, may we walk only in the light of Your Divine Son. Help Your people to always follow His teachings and deny the evil one.*

—————————

 AM the Resurrection and the life. Whoever believes in Me, even though he dies, will live, and everyone who lives and believes in Me will never die.

MAR.

7

—Jn 11:25-26

REFLECTION. As we see so many reminders of the dead of winter around us, still our hearts are filled with hope for the springtime of life that is sure to come.

For believers that new life can be forever.

PRAYER. *God, our Father, the Lord Jesus promised to go from this earth to prepare a place for each of us. May we persevere in good, spurred on by the Resurrection.*

NOW is the acceptable time; behold, now is the day of salvation.

—2 Cor 6:2

REFLECTION. Each day, we progress in our determination to become more closely united with Christ, especially in His Passion and Death.

Thus, we are living the salvation so dearly earned for us on Calvary.

PRAYER. *Holy Lord, Your Divine Son hung between heaven and earth that we might live forever. May we always walk in the shadow of that holy Cross.*

 THE words that I have spoken to you are spirit and life.

—Jn 6:63

REFLECTION. Created in the image and likeness of God, we search our genealogy in Scripture.

As we embrace God's Word, we are guided by the Holy Spirit and led into the light of God's presence.

PRAYER. *Father, Creator of heaven and earth, we open ourselves to Your Spirit that we may walk always in the light. Grant us the grace never to falter in our search for truth and life.*

HE Lord is my shepherd; there is nothing I shall lack. He makes me lie down in green pastures; He leads me to tranquil streams. He restores my soul.

—Ps 23:1-3

REFLECTION. In the midst of challenging and troubling times, God's Word soothes and strokes us with a gentle reminder of the peace and quiet that come from our God.

We long to settle near His life-giving waters.

PRAYER. *Heavenly Father, through Your Son, Jesus Christ, we have been signed with Your greeting of peace. May we, with Your help, bring peace into our lives and the lives of all those we meet in this life.*

 ABANDONED you for a brief moment, but with great compassion I will take you back.

—Isa 54:7

REFLECTION. Although we have offended our God, He holds no grudge.

In our personal relationships, we join in the creation of a new earth by removing any vindictiveness from our hearts.

PRAYER. *God, our Father, as we turn back to You, seeking Your compassion and love, help us to avoid any semblance of revenge in word or action.*

JESUS said to him, "Unless you witness signs and wonders, you will not believe." —Jn 4:48

MAR.
12

REFLECTION. As part of our conversion process, we reflect on the many talents, gifts, and graces that have come into our lives.

In simple faith we acknowledge our total dependence on God and divest ourselves of wants.

PRAYER. *Merciful Father, in this flood time of grace, we praise You especially for the gift of Faith. May we strengthen our belief during times of trial and temptation.*

THUS says the Lord of hosts: The fast of the fourth, the fifth, the seventh, and the tenth months are to be days of joy and gladness, cheerful festivals for the house of Judah; therefore love faithfulness and peace. —Zec 8:19

MAR.
13

REFLECTION. As we make our Lenten fast, we carry through with joy and great cheer in the knowledge that we are turning toward God.

Our God is a God of peace and love with which He embraces us.

PRAYER. *O Lord, our God, we seek always to live in Your peace and love. May we abstain from any conduct that would lead us into sin.*

ND Moses went into the cloud and up on the mountain. There he stayed for forty days and forty nights.

MAR.
14

—Ex 24:18

REFLECTION. On mountaintop, plain, or at sea level, we pass through the cloud of indifference and neglect in order to become closer and closer to the Lord.

We build up those graces that we have lost through our backsliding.

PRAYER. *Heavenly Father, we come to You, conscious of having left behind all worldly attachments. In our time with You, let us think only of Your great love for us.*

 AVID pleaded with God for the child. He fasted and spent the night on the ground clothed in sackcloth.

MAR.
15

—2 Sam 12:16

REFLECTION. In our turning back to God to seek His forgiveness for our past sins, we abstain from those "creature comforts" to which we have become attached.

We fast in memory of the Lord's Suffering and Death.

PRAYER. *Merciful Lord, hear our prayers of supplication as we cry out for forgiveness of our failures. May we always turn to You in time of temptation and sin.*

HE got up and ate and drank; strengthened by that food, he walked forty days and forty nights to Horeb, the mountain of God. —1 Ki 19:8

MAR.
16

REFLECTION. Nourished by the Body and Blood of Christ, we walk to the mountain of God, both in joy and fasting.

Our forty days and nights are the springtime of our salvation.

PRAYER. *Lord, our God, be with us as we walk toward the celebration of Your Son's Death and Resurrection. May our fast be pleasing in Your sight and beneficial to our neighbor.*

HE fasted for forty days and forty nights, after which He was famished. —Mt 4:2

MAR.
17

REFLECTION. As we maintain our Lenten fast, we long to be filled with the graces of God.

We hunger for the coming of the Spirit to fill us with the wisdom of the Lord and set us on fire with His love.

PRAYER. *Lord God, free Your people from any faults or attachments that would offend You. May we always walk in Your light, free from even the slightest sin.*

YET, when they were ill, I put on sackcloth and afflicted myself with fasting, while I poured forth prayers from my heart. —Ps 35:13

REFLECTION. As we cleanse ourselves from sin and pride during the Lenten season, one of our greatest challenges is being Christlike with those who see themselves as our enemies, or those who are disdainful of us.

We fast and pray for them.

PRAYER. *Father, Your Son, Jesus Christ, preached Your Word and many opposed Him. May we always follow Christ in the gentle and understanding way He loved His opponents.*

HER husband Joseph was a just man and did not wish to expose her to the ordeal of public disgrace; therefore, he resolved to divorce her quietly. —Mt 1:19

REFLECTION. We strive to imitate the strength of Joseph's convictions.

We seek out his qualities of gentleness and compassion, avoiding at all costs, in any way, embarrassing our friends and relatives.

PRAYER. *God, our Father, You have given us a great model in Joseph, foster father of Your Divine Son. May we strive to live his quiet and virtuous lifestyle.*

I AM fading away like an evening shadow; I am shaken off like a locust.

—Ps 109:23

REFLECTION. When the locusts come, their song makes a very deep impression. Suddenly, the music stops and they are gone.

This process of nature helps us understand our own lives. In an instant we are gone, but hopefully we go into God's presence.

PRAYER. *Lord, our God, we pray for the grace to persevere in good. May we take advantage of Your grace and Word.*

 DENYING the Lord, they said, "Not He. No evil will come upon us; we shall see neither sword nor famine."

—Jer 5:12

REFLECTION. Sometimes, using the gifts that God has given us, we may become successful in worldly things and begin to see ourselves as invincible.

This kind of trap must be avoided at all costs through prayer and detachment.

PRAYER. *Loving Father, in Your care and concern, You have made us in Your image and likeness. May we always reflect Your goodness and dispel any pride that may come into our lives.*

FOR just as the Father has life in Himself, so also He has granted the Son to have life in Himself. —Jn 5:26

MAR. 22

REFLECTION. God, the Father of all life, sent us His Son, fully possessed of the life shared with the Father. We are invited to share in that life by enhancing all life that God has given the world.

To defend life is to defend the Lord.

PRAYER. *God, our Father, You created us out of nothing and breathed life into us, sharing with us Your eternal Being. May we always respect every form of life that is with, in, and through You.*

 THE Lord said to Moses, "I see how stiff-necked this people is. Leave me alone; my wrath will blaze up against them. But of you I will make a great nation." —Ex 32:9-10

MAR. 23

REFLECTION. Offenses against God have a negative effect on our society.

Truly good citizens of any nation make a solid contribution to their country through lives of virtue.

PRAYER. *O Lord, be mindful of Your people who strive to do Your Will. Strengthen us that we may truly live as citizens destined for heaven.*

THEN Jesus cried out as He was teaching in the temple, "You know Me, and you also know where I am from. Yet I have not come of My own accord, but He Who sent Me is true. You do not know Him, but I know Him because I am from Him and it was He Who sent Me." **MAR. 24**

—Jn 7:28-29

REFLECTION. Our Lord preached repentance and forgiveness.

The solid foundation of His teaching, based on His relationship with God, the Father, is enough for us to respond to conversion with all our hearts.

PRAYER. *God, our Father, save us from our pride and lead us into the light of faith in the teachings of Your Son, Jesus. May we remain His faithful followers.*

HE was contemplating their destruction, but Moses, His chosen one, stood in the breach before Him to keep His wrath from destroying them. —Ps 106:23 **MAR. 25**

REFLECTION. We are so blessed in having Mary, the one chosen to be the mother of the Son of God, as our intercessor.

When we deserve God's wrath, or find ourselves in any difficulty, we go to her for protection.

PRAYER. *Heavenly Father, we acknowledge our weaknesses and doubts. Let us always turn to Mary in time of temptation and grief, knowing You will accept her word for us.*

AND you will know that I am the **MAR.** Lord, when I open your graves and raise you from them, O My people.

26

—Ezek 37:13

REFLECTION. The culmination of a life of holiness in the Lord will see us spring from our graves and be taken up with the Lord.

The fast and penance of our Lent pale in comparison.

PRAYER. *Lord of all creation, You free us from sin so that we might overcome death and the grave. May Your Second Coming be ever on our minds each day in our prayer.*

NO one else was present, aside from **MAR.** the two elders who were watching her from their concealed hiding place.

27

—Dan 13:16

REFLECTION. The two elders who lusted after Susanna paid with their lives for their indulgence in unbridled passion.

It is better for us to avert our eyes from any temptation rather than fall into the death of sin.

PRAYER. *O Lord, our God, may we always walk in the light of purity and truth. Let us not cave into any fancy for a few moments of fleshly pleasure that could destroy us.*

WHEN this man heard that Jesus had come from Judea to Galilee, he went to Him and pleaded that He come and heal his son who was near death. —Jn 4:47

MAR. 28

REFLECTION. In faith, we turn in prayer to the Lord Jesus in all our needs, especially our concern to be healed of our sins.

We ask Jesus to save us from the death and destruction of sin.

PRAYER. *Lord God, through the merits of Your Son's Crucifixion and Death, heal us of all our sins and our tendency to wander into the occasion of sin. May we strive to lead upright lives.*

ONLY goodness and kindness will follow me all the days of my life, and I will dwell in the house of the Lord forever and ever. —Ps 23:6

MAR. 29

REFLECTION. Quietly we mull over in our minds God's goodness and His invitation to live with Him forever.

Every detachment and penance of our conversion suddenly seems well worthwhile.

PRAYER. *Merciful and gracious Lord, our spirits look forward to be united in Your presence forever. Our humanity draws us back and suggests that we hesitate. May we remove all doubts and hesitation.*

TAKE no part in the fruitless deeds of darkness, but rather seek to expose them. For it is shameful even to speak of what deeds people do in secret.

MAR.
30

—Eph 5:11-12

REFLECTION. Jesus, our Shepherd, is light. We strive to deepen virtue in our lives and walk always in the light of Christ.

Our thoughts, words, and deeds are lived in such a way as to dispel any notion of secrecy.

PRAYER. *God, our Father, in Your great goodness, You call us to be Your children. Let us never fail to consciously live as Your sons and daughters.*

FOR I am about to create new heavens and a new earth; the past shall not be remembered or come to mind.

MAR.
31

—Isa 65:17

REFLECTION. We are called to be a people of hope. Through God's grace we become a new people.

All that we have been in the past is washed away in the Blood of the Lamb. Neither we nor God will remember our sins.

PRAYER. *Lord God, You create us in Your image and likeness and renew us and save us from ourselves. May we always remain faithful to Your commands and Your love.*

HEREVER the river goes, every living creature that multiplies shall live, and there shall be numerous fish. Wherever this water goes it brings life. —Ezek 47:9

REFLECTION. Life-giving water will flow out of God's holy temple.

For us, the temple is the Body of Christ, hanging on the Cross, waiting to be pierced. It is from that wound that the water of salvation flows.

PRAYER. *God, our Father, Your Son, Jesus Christ, cleanses us from our sins by the Blood and water shed on His Cross. Let us always remember His great sacrifice.*

EITHER do I condemn you," Jesus said. "Go on your way, and sin no more." —Jn 8:11

REFLECTION. No matter how long we have been recognized as sinners, Jesus constantly asks us if we want to be free of our sins.

At any moment, we can offer our contrition and plan to amend our lives as best we can.

PRAYER. *Loving God, You look with great compassion on us sinners. Help us to hasten to the forgiveness won for us on the Cross.*

THEY shall not hunger or thirst, neither shall scorching wind nor sun strike them; for He Who pities them will lead them and guide them by springs of water. —Isa 49:10

REFLECTION. Like the prophets of old, we have to remind ourselves from time to time how great God's love is for us.

The people who heard the prophets did not experience Jesus as we do. All the more reason for us to return God's great love in thought, word, and deed.

PRAYER. *God, our Father, You ordain that we be baptized with living water. May we always be living water and life for others.*

THEY forgot the God Who had saved them, Who had done great things in Egypt, wonders in the land of Ham, and awesome deeds at the Red Sea. —Ps 106:21-22

REFLECTION. One of the realities of conversion is the realization we have turned our back on God every time that we slide back into sin.

We turn aside the wrath of God by our penance and sorrow.

PRAYER. *Lord God, as we contemplate all the gifts and graces You have given, we are saddened by our indifference and neglect. Prepare us to rise from our sins and to celebrate Your Resurrection.*

HY should the Egyptians say, "With evil intent He brought them out to kill them in the mountains and wipe them off the face of the earth"? Let Your fierce wrath subside; relent and do not bring wrath on Your people. —Ex 32:12

APR. 5

REFLECTION. The anger of the Lord has been consumed in the sacrifice of Jesus on Calvary.

We are forgiven and must resolve never to turn away from God again.

PRAYER. *Father Almighty, Your Son, Jesus, paid the supreme sacrifice with His life that we might be saved from our sins and live. May our lives reflect Jesus' love.*

OT that I accept such human testimony, but I say these things so that you may be saved. John was a burning and shining lamp, and for a time you were willing to exult in his light. —Jn 5:34-35

APR. 6

REFLECTION. We take our Lenten resolutions seriously.

We embrace the Baptist's cry for reform and repentance. We persevere in good and spice our daily lives with some detachment.

PRAYER. *Lord God, Your people accept Your invitation to convert and reform. May we continue to live resolutely with Your Divine help.*

ET us see if what they say is true, and let us probe what will happen at the conclusion of their life. For if those who are just are God's children, He will defend them and deliver them from the power of their enemies. —Wis 2:17-18

APR. 7

REFLECTION. The plotting by Jesus' enemies portends the great tragedy of the Cross.

They were so close to the truth and refused to accept it, but were willing to test it and take a chance with the big "if."

PRAYER. *Lord God, Your words are truth and light. May we always seek truth in Your words and Your Will in our regard.*

 O they tried to arrest Him, but no one laid a hand upon Him because His hour had not yet come. —Jn 7:30

APR. 8

REFLECTION. The reality of the truth that Jesus taught and spoke infuriated His enemies. Even today, followers of Jesus upset neighbors by their loving lifestyle.

Yet to live in love and peace with one another is God's truth.

PRAYER. *Loving Father, may we always be brothers and sisters for one another, steeped in Your great love for us.*

THE righteous call out, and the Lord hears them; He rescues them from all their troubles. —Ps 34:18

REFLECTION. As we make our journey, walking always in the light of Christ, we know that the Lord will be with us.

He will guard us from the attacks of the evil one.

PRAYER. *Lord, our God, in faith we turn to You in our need. Hear the prayers of Your faithful and keep us in Your love.*

THE Lord God helps Me, so I am not disgraced. I have set My face like flint because I know that I shall not be put to shame. —Isa 50:7

REFLECTION. Isaiah's words reflect the strength and determination of our Lord in the face of those who were plotting to put Him to death.

As we deal with the threat of death through sin, we seek our strength in Jesus.

PRAYER. *Almighty Father, be with us as we live our day-to-day struggle to walk always in the light. May we turn to Jesus, Mary, and Joseph in times of trial.*

THROUGH the evidence of such service, you are giving glory to God for your obedient profession of the Gospel of Christ. **APR. 11**

—2 Cor 9:13

REFLECTION. Our God does not demand that we die on a cross.

But He does require of us the obedience of Jesus to His Commandments.

PRAYER. *God, our Father, help us to embrace Your Word and Your Law. May we imitate Jesus in conforming our wills to Yours.*

———————————

 YOU came near when I called to You; You said, "Do not be afraid!" **APR. 12**

—Lam 3:57

REFLECTION. Nothing else matters in our lives but our relationship with God.

Once we are straight with God, we have nothing to fear here and now or hereafter.

PRAYER. *We come to You, Father, with great hope and expectation. Be with us in all that we do so that we may live according to Your wishes.*

HE poor you will always have with you, but you will not always have Me.

APR. 13

—Jn 12:8

REFLECTION. One of the underlying themes of Jesus' public teaching is the fundamental option for the poor.

That we will always have the poor with us is an assurance of opportunity to both imitate and accomplish Christ's work.

PRAYER. *Merciful Lord, we turn to You that we might be freed from our sin. As You share Your forgiveness with us, may we share our gifts and talents with Your poor.*

E to me a rock of refuge to which I can always go; proclaim the order to save me, for You are my rock and my fortress.

APR. 14

—Ps 71:3

REFLECTION. As we look for defense and security in our lives, we turn to the Lord God for protection from the evil one.

Although many calamities may befall us, the only thing that matters is that we are intimate with the Lord.

PRAYER. *God in heaven, we seek Your care and protection every day. May the Angels and Saints be with us in our struggle with temptation.*

THEN one of the Twelve, the man called Judas Iscariot, went to the chief priests and asked, "What are you willing to give me if I hand Him over to you?" They paid him thirty pieces of silver.

APR. 15

—Mt 26:14-15

REFLECTION. Every time we entertain the tempter, we turn our backs on Jesus. We betray Him.

We can be blinded by the glitter of the particular silver for which we reach.

PRAYER. *God, our Creator, we are all too aware of our human weakness. Help us not to be deceived by the wealth and power of this world.*

———————

CLOTHE the heavens in black, and make sackcloth their covering. —Isa 50:3

APR. 16

REFLECTION. When Jesus expired on the Cross, the heavens were torn asunder, and lightning brightened the skies.

In the realization that our sins contributed to His terrible death, we resolve to seek only our needs not our wants.

PRAYER. *God of mercy and judgment, help us to understand that we are made only for You. Help us to shed all trappings of worldliness.*

HAVE become alienated from my brothers, a stranger to my mother's sons. Zeal for Your house consumes me, and the insults directed at You fall on me. —Ps 69:9-10

APR. 17

REFLECTION. We are well aware of the personal attacks on Jesus during His public life, given the substance of His preaching.

Today, in memory of our Lord, we willingly embrace the ridicule, questioning, and anger against our faith community.

PRAYER. *All-powerful God, in Your great wisdom, You permit vicious attacks on the barque of Peter. May we always remain steadfast in faith and silent in the midst of humiliations.*

 HE Son of Man indeed goes, as it is written of Him, but woe to that man by whom the Son of Man is betrayed. It would be better for that man if he had never been born. —Mt 26:24

APR. 18

REFLECTION. We know that Jesus went to His death on the Cross. We are overjoyed that He rose from the dead.

Now, as we walk in the valley of death, we are assured that the risen Lord will come back to take us to Himself in the land of the living.

PRAYER. *Almighty God, we hope and trust in You, knowing that Your promises will be kept. May we always live as to be worthy of Your Word.*

UT God raised Him to life on the third day and allowed Him to be seen not by all the people but by witnesses who were chosen by God in advance—by us who ate and drank with Him after He rose from the dead. —Acts 10:40-41

REFLECTION. The Resurrection of Jesus is so assuring on many levels. He ate and drank with the disciples.

He invites us to eat and drink here with Him, something the Angels may not do.

PRAYER. *Jesus, risen from the dead, we rejoice in Your being with us in the breaking of the Bread. May we always prepare ourselves worthily for this banquet.*

IVE thanks to the Lord, for He is good; for His kindness endures forever. —Ps 118:1

REFLECTION. The enduring mercy of God through Jesus Christ should be for us a source of endless joy.

While we walk with feet of clay, we know that we need but turn to the Lord during the first moment of a slip from grace.

PRAYER. *Father of mercy, we walk in the light of Your goodness. Forgive our faults that we might be with You forever.*

OME of our companions went to the tomb and found everything exactly as the women had said, but they did not see Him. —Lk 24:24

REFLECTION. In hope, the disciples rushed to the scene of Jesus' burial. They did not find Him.

We are blessed in the knowledge that He has risen, and that we have the opportunity to never die again.

PRAYER. *God, our Father, we rejoice in the Good News that Christ rose from the tomb to bring life and light to all nations. May we always be a source of hope, light, and peace for others.*

 OWEVER, God raised Him up, releasing Him from the pangs of death, because it was impossible for Him to be held in its power. —Acts 2:24

REFLECTION. The raising of Jesus from death reminds us of our destiny.

With the grace of God we will overcome sin and temptation and avoid eternal death.

PRAYER. *Lord God, we rejoice in the Resurrection of Christ from the dead. May our lives always reflect His Resurrection that we might live in His glory forever.*

HEN Jesus said to them, "Do not be fearful. Go and tell My brethren to go to Galilee. There they will see Me."

APR. 23

—Mt 28:10

REFLECTION. As brothers and sisters in the Lord, we make haste to answer Jesus' invitation to go to Galilee.

Every day we are on the road, seeking His presence and cultivating our personal holiness.

PRAYER. *Lord, our God, You sent Your Son, Jesus Christ, to redeem us. Let us always walk toward Him in the light of the Resurrection.*

HEN Jesus approached them and said, "All authority in heaven and on earth has been given to Me. Go, therefore, and make disciples of all nations, baptizing them in the name of the Father and of the Son and of the Holy Spirit."

APR. 24

—Mt 28:18-19

REFLECTION. Far away from Galilee, we realize that Jesus had us in mind when He sent the disciples through their successors.

Our baptism gave us the keys to the Kingdom. We need guard them with great care.

PRAYER. *God, our Father, help us to own the miracle of Jesus' Resurrection. On the path to salvation, may we live out our baptismal promises.*

THIS is the day that the Lord has made; let us exult and rejoice in it.

—Ps 118:24

APR. 25

REFLECTION. Every dawn reminds us that God is in control of the universe.

As the followers of Christ, we rejoice in God's care for us each day of our lives and share that joy with all.

PRAYER. *Almighty God and Father of light, we rejoice in the life that You have given us. Help us never to stray from Your Will, which brings happiness.*

 THOSE who accepted His message were baptized, and on that day about three thousand people were added to their number.

—Acts 2:41

APR. 26

REFLECTION. Through our baptism we become heralds of the Lord's message of salvation.

Like Peter, we speak not only words but perform actions to bring the Good News of salvation to our friends and neighbors.

PRAYER. *Lord God, we serve You in faith and joy. May we live our lives in order to bring others to the truth and light.*

WHEN He was at table with them, He took bread, blessed and broke it, and gave it to them. Then their eyes were opened and they recognized Him, but He vanished from their sight. —Lk 24:30-31

APR. 27

REFLECTION. When we share the Eucharist with one another, we are assured that Jesus will never depart from us.

Hence, we pray every day for a deeper faith in the Blessed Sacrament.

PRAYER. *Almighty God, we praise and thank You for the memorial gift Jesus left us. May we receive Him with great reverence and profound respect.*

 WHILE they were still conversing about this, Jesus Himself stood in their midst and said to them, "Peace be with you." —Lk 24:36

APR. 28

REFLECTION. The risen Christ speaks of peace to the entire universe.

While the world may never seem at peace, our walking with the Lord in all things gives us deep serenity.

PRAYER. *Father of Peace, we give You thanks and praise for accepting us into Your peace. May we be peace for others, especially our families.*

LORD, our Lord, how glorious is Your Name in all the earth! You have exalted Your majesty above the heavens. —Ps 8:2

APR. 29

REFLECTION. God's power and heavenly exaltation are beautifully and clearly seen in the Resurrection.

We share in the very life of the exalted Lord through pure minds and hearts.

PRAYER. *Eternal Father, we come to You in humility, asking that You hear our petitions. May our lives, filled with Your grace, be worthy of Your Kingdom.*

 HILE they were still speaking to the people, the priests, the captain of the temple guard, and the Sadducees came over to them, greatly annoyed that they were teaching and proclaiming to the people the resurrection of the dead through Jesus. —Acts 4:1-2

APR. 30

REFLECTION. We speak to all peoples when we proclaim the right to life for the born, the unborn, and the terminally ill.

We proclaim Jesus' Resurrection in our fundamental option for the poor.

PRAYER. *Father of love and mercy, guide us as we bring Your message of love and mercy to the poor and rejected. Let us bring quality of life to as many as possible.*

N the sixth month, the Angel Gabriel was
sent by God to a town in Galilee called
Nazareth, to a virgin betrothed to a man
named Joseph, of the house of David. The
virgin's name was Mary. —Lk 1:26-27

MAY

1

REFLECTION. As we enter Mary's month, the
very beginning of Mary's relationship with
the Church calls to mind the beauty of our
faith in the person of the mother of God.

From the instant of the Angel's visit, the
name Mary will be for all eternity.

PRAYER. *Father of love and mercy, in the person of Your Divine Son's mother, we have a great treasure. May we always turn to Mary in times of trial.*

———————

 ARY said, "Behold, I am the servant of the Lord. Let it be done to
me according to your word." After
this, the Angel departed from her.
—Lk 1:38

MAY

2

REFLECTION. Like Mary, we open ourselves up
to the Father's Will in our regard.

In simplicity, and without attachments, we
live our lives according to the Word of the
Lord.

PRAYER. *Eternal Father, in many ways You
show us Your desire for us to live according to
Your plan. May we always seek to do Your
Will in union with Mary.*

IS mother said to the servants, "Do whatever He tells you." —Jn 2:5

MAY 3

REFLECTION. A mother knows her son's mind and heart. She knows the special ways to reach him.

What a wonderful intercessor we have in heaven in the person of Mary.

PRAYER. *We praise and glorify You, Almighty and ever-loving God, for the wonderful intercessor we have in the person of Mary, the mother of Your Divine Son. Help us to be close to Jesus on earth as she was.*

 HE birth of Jesus Christ occurred in this way. When His mother Mary was engaged to Joseph, but before they came to live together, she was found to be with Child through the Holy Spirit.

—Mt 1:18

MAY 4

REFLECTION. What faith Mary and Joseph had to exercise before the full reality of the Incarnation was grasped.

Like Mary and Joseph, our faith must be strong as we confront the challenges of modern life.

PRAYER. *Almighty and eternal God, Your plan for our salvation could happen only through the faith of Mary and Joseph. We ask Your care as we strive to deepen our faith in Your Word.*

HOEVER does the Will of My heavenly Father is My brother and sister and mother.

MAY 5

—Mt 12:50

REFLECTION. We come to many crossroads in our spiritual lives.

We choose prayer over laziness; love over disdain; charity over stinginess; purity over sensuality and thus become sister, brother, and mother to Jesus.

PRAYER. *God of love, we praise You for the integrity of Your family to which You call us. With Mary's help, may we choose the greater good and be inscribed in the register of life.*

 HEN His mother and His brethren arrived, looking for Him, but they could not get near Him because of the crowd.

MAY 6

—Lk 8:19

REFLECTION. Mary, our model, was anxious to hear what Jesus taught during His public life.

We too seek out the Word of the Lord in Scripture, preaching, and Church teachings.

PRAYER. *Father of all goodness, help us to imitate Mary in living out the Word of Your Son. Keep us always in Your care and close to Mary.*

N the third day, there was a wedding at Cana in Galilee. The mother of Jesus was there. —Jn 2:1

MAY 7

REFLECTION. Like ordinary folks, Mary and Jesus were invited to a wedding.

In all the important occasions of our lives, we would do well to have Mary with us both in prayer and circumstances.

PRAYER. *Father of everlasting goodness, we rejoice in the role of the mother of Jesus, Your Son. May we always seek her counsel and guidance.*

 HEN Jesus saw His mother and the disciple whom He loved standing beside her, He said to His mother, "Woman, behold, your son."

MAY 8

—Jn 19:26

REFLECTION. As sisters and brothers in Christ, we all have a common mother in Mary.

It is important that we become aware of the fullness of Mary's concern and compassion for her children.

PRAYER. *Ever-loving God, we give You thanks and praise for allowing Mary to be our intercessor and protector. Like Jesus, may we always walk with her.*

NE night, the Lord appeared to Paul in a vision and said, "Do not be afraid. Continue with your preaching, and do not be silent."

MAY 9

—Acts 18:9

REFLECTION. As Christians living in an age of deceit and untruth, we may not be silent. We speak for life, truth, peace, justice, the elderly, the sick and poor.

We accept ridicule as an outcome of proclaiming our beliefs.

PRAYER. *God, our Father and Protector, be with us as we stand firm in the face of opposition that would have us give up our convictions. May we gently accept corresponding criticism.*

———————

LESSED are the merciful, for they will obtain mercy. —Mt 5:7

MAY 10

REFLECTION. As we go about our daily lives, Jesus' public life and teachings are a constant reminder for us.

They help us to assuage, to the best of our ability, little injustices that we come across every day.

PRAYER. *Merciful and just Lord, be with us as we seek to live out Your justice in our lives. May we always protect the interests of the weak and rejected.*

MEN, amen, I say to you, you will weep and mourn while the world rejoices. You will be sorrowful, but your grief will turn into joy.

—Jn 16:20

REFLECTION. Many times our joy and happiness are at odds with what is worldly. Moreover, worldly joys may inflict disappointment and rejection.

We know through faith that our joy will never be overcome.

PRAYER. *Father of everlasting goodness, in joy and peace we walk in Your light. In times of trial, may we never lose hope.*

E said: "Truly they are My people, children who will not deal falsely"; He became their Savior in all their troubles. —Isa 63:8

REFLECTION. One of the greatest afflictions we suffer in this life is a tendency toward and giving into sin.

Still, we go on, confident in the love and grace of God in our regard.

PRAYER. *Unchanging God, through Your Son, Jesus Christ, we have been given the gift of salvation. Help us never to squander Your gift on the wickedness of the world.*

AY God rise up, and His enemies be scattered; may His foes flee before Him. —Ps 68:2

REFLECTION. When we stick to the Lord, we will have no trouble from the enemies of God.

Keeping the presence of God in mind is a beneficial form of prayer.

PRAYER. *God of power and life, be with us as we seek out Your Will each day. May we stay close to Jesus and His mother at all times.*

 LESSED be the Lord, day after day, the God of our salvation, Who carries our burden. —Ps 68:20

REFLECTION. Daily we lift our minds and hearts to God in a wonderful exchange of love.

This love is rooted in the assurance of God's presence with us to the very end.

PRAYER. *Father of wisdom, guide us in Your way. Watch over us that we may walk in Your presence at all times.*

HOVER humbles himself and becomes like this child is the greatest in the Kingdom of Heaven. And whoever receives one such child in My Name receives Me. —Mt 18:4-5

MAY 15

REFLECTION. We all owe a great debt to our teachers, especially those who trained us in the Faith.

They received us in God's Name and will be received by the Lord.

PRAYER. *Father, You remind us that those who instruct others unto justice will shine like stars for all eternity. We ask Your blessing on all our teachers, living and deceased.*

 N the following night, the Lord appeared to Paul and said, "Keep up your courage! For just as you have borne witness to Me in Jerusalem, so you must also bear witness in Rome." —Acts 23:11

MAY 16

REFLECTION. Clearly, the old adage, "When in Rome, do as the Romans do," cannot be part of our tradition when it comes to faith matters.

Wherever we find ourselves, we carry the true Faith with us, always respectful of local custom, except in matters that violate our beliefs.

PRAYER. *Almighty Father, when Mary fled with Jesus and Joseph into Egypt, the Holy Family remained faithful to the Kingdom. May we imitate their courage and faith.*

HERE are also many other things that Jesus did; and if every one of them was recorded, I do not think the world itself could contain the books that would be written. —Jn 21:25

REFLECTION. The unrecorded goodness of Jesus while on earth is a clarion call for His followers to seek out and assist those who are less gifted and talented.

In reaching out to the marginalized, we are sure to find Jesus, perhaps where we least expect.

PRAYER. *God, our Father and Protector, You call us to holiness through Your grace and good works. May we be guardians of the poor and outcast. Help us be their voice.*

HE Lord tests the upright and the wicked; He detests the lover of violence. —Ps 11:5

REFLECTION. We are not naturally given to violence. Anger and real or false hurt can build up within us if we allow it to do so. But at what price?

As brothers and sisters of Jesus, we do all in our power to live the patience and charity of Christ. Our first choice is to avoid God's wrath.

PRAYER. *Father of peace, may we be Your sons and daughters of peace. Remove all impatience and revenge from our lives. Help us to share Your peace with all people.*

HEY were all astounded and perplexed, and they said to one another, "What does all this mean?" However, others said mockingly, "They are filled with new wine." —Acts 2:12-13

MAY 19

REFLECTION. The onlookers who gathered because of the sound of the great wind on Pentecost Sunday were both surprised and delighted to hear the Galilean disciples speaking to them in their tongue.

The universal language we speak on behalf of Jesus is that of love, peace, and justice.

PRAYER. *Father of everlasting goodness, be with us as we bring Your Word into our lives and share it with others. May we speak to them in terms of Your loving forgiveness.*

 O each of us, the manifestation of the Spirit is given for the common good. —1 Cor 12:7

MAY 20

REFLECTION. The Holy Spirit of God comes to each of us in a very special way, suitable only for us. Our talents and goodwill merge in the Spirit for the honor and glory of God.

Assured that we are in the Lord, we set out on life's task with the enthusiasm of the early disciples.

PRAYER. *Almighty God and Father of light, we celebrate Your Spirit's presence with us and within us and in one another. May we always be strengthened with Your abiding presence and bring us to unity with You forever.*

FTER saying this, He breathed on them and said, "Receive the Holy Spirit. If you forgive anyone's sins, they are forgiven. If you retain anyone's sins, they are retained." —Jn 20:22-23

MAY 21

REFLECTION. An Irish lad told a Jewish boy, "Our priest knows much more than your rabbi." The Jewish lad said, "Of course he does, you tell him everything."

How important to tell everything in Confession, where instant forgiveness is available through the merits of Jesus Christ.

PRAYER. *Unchanging God, Your promise of forgiveness enlightens our way on the road to our heavenly home. May we always be honest and forthright in making our Confessions.*

 NSTEAD, what you ought to say is, "If it is the Lord's Will, we shall live to do this or that." —Jas 4:15

MAY 22

REFLECTION. We give over our lives completely to God.

Practicality calls for planning in each life. We make our plans and schedules, always aware that they come about only if it is according to God's schedule for us.

PRAYER. *Lord, our God, we give You thanks and praise for the great gifts of life and salvation. May we always be aware that all we do in this life depends on Your Will for us.*

HOEVER gives you a cup of water to drink because you bear the Name of Christ will certainly not go unrewarded. —Mk 9:41

MAY 23

REFLECTION. Our call to charity is universal. So many people depend on our generosity, not necessarily from a monetary point of view, but from the spiritual side.

Our example can save a person's soul.

PRAYER. *Almighty and eternal God, we seek to do Your Will in bringing others to Your salvation. Help us live our lives in the fullness of Your commands so that others may see and come to believe.*

 BOVE all, my brethren, do not swear, either by heaven or by earth, or use any oaths at all. Let your "Yes" mean "Yes" and your "No" mean "No." Otherwise you may be condemned. —Jas 5:12

MAY 24

REFLECTION. James' words to speak only the truth and do it in a straightforward way are very appropriate for our time. Speaking with courage while being forthright allows us to speak with a clear conscience.

At the same time, mutual respect and fidelity in all interpersonal relations are preserved. Unvarnished truth is a breath of fresh air in our world.

PRAYER. *Father, Author of all truth, help us to speak the truth at all times, never swearing to any questionable statements. May our love for You enhance our respect for all people.*

THEREFORE, confess your sins to one another and pray for one another, so that you may be healed. The prayer of a righteous man is powerful and effective. —Jas 5:16

MAY 25

REFLECTION. At every Mass, we publicly proclaim our sinfulness to God and to one another.

This can be an exercise in humility; yet, at the same time, it can be a periodic examination of conscience, enabling us to live virtuously.

PRAYER. *Merciful Father, as we recall the memorial of Your Son's Death and Resurrection, we lay out our sins and faults. We accept Your invitation to forgiveness, and ask Your care in keeping our minds and hearts pure.*

WHEN Jesus became aware of this, He was indignant and said to them, "Let the little children come to Me; do not hinder them. For it is to such as these that the Kingdom of God belongs." —Mk 10:14

MAY 26

REFLECTION. The Lord looks to parents and guardians to show children His love and how to live out His Commandments.

The Lord demands from the Church that care be taken to provide them necessary instruction and help in receiving the Sacraments. These are the key to their salvation.

PRAYER. *God of all compassion, Your Son, Jesus, shows us how to be present to our children. May we always love them enough to be with them in seeking the Lord's way.*

OR my eyes have seen Your salvation, which You have prepared in the sight of all the peoples. —Lk 2:30-31

MAY 27

REFLECTION. When God sent Jesus to save us, His salvation was meant for all peoples of all ages. The very fact that all are invited can be a source of unity.

To speak of and act on ethnic differences is not only foolish but mocks God's love for His people.

PRAYER. *God of power and life, in Your great goodness, You desire all people to have eternal life. May we never allow individual differences to influence our actions toward anyone.*

 LTHOUGH you have not seen Him, you love Him; and even though you do not see Him now, you believe in Him and are filled with a joy that is indescribable and glorious. —1 Pet 1:8

MAY 28

REFLECTION. Although called to be a people of joy, we understand that our joy is based on faith. We believe in God's love for all His people.

We believe that, like Mary, He has our best interests at heart. We believe it is best to do the Lord's Will.

PRAYER. *Almighty Father, You ask us to believe without seeing and to pray without ceasing. Help us to strengthen our faith by adhering to the duties of our state in life as did Mary.*

REAT are the works of the Lord; they are pondered by all who delight in them. —Ps 111:2

REFLECTION. How appropriate that May is dedicated to our Mother Mary. In the full blossoming of spring we have a reflection of Mary's beauty and goodness.

Our spirits are lifted by God's creation and Mary's role in our salvation.

PRAYER. *Father of all holiness, may the beauty of spring lead us to admire and imitate the beauty of Mary's holiness. In times of difficulty, may we always turn to her as our intercessor.*

 HE disciples were even more greatly astonished, and they said to one another, "Then who can be saved?" Jesus looked at them and said, "For men it is impossible, but not for God. For God all things are possible." —Mk 10:26-27

REFLECTION. How consoling are Jesus' words. Even for the most wretched of individuals, a slight turn toward the Lord, and the miracle of salvation is accomplished.

When we help the most desperate, we have an assurance of God's power in accepting and forgiving all.

PRAYER. *Lord God, our Savior, You seek us out in the deepest dens of our iniquities. You are the Light leading us up from the slavery of sin. Grant us the grace always to return to Your house.*

ET your love be sincere. Loathe what is evil and hold fast to what is good. Love one another with genuine affection. Esteem others more highly than yourself. **MAY 31**

—Rom 12:9-10

REFLECTION. God's inspired Word proves to be a perfect design for interpersonal relationships. Called to be a people of peace, living in honor, respect, mutual concern and good, these are ingredients for a near utopia.

It emulates the hospitality and affection Elizabeth gave Mary when she visited.

PRAYER. *Father of peace, be with us as we bring the Good News of salvation to a troubled world. Like Mary, may we reach out to others in time of need.*

 LESS the Lord, O my soul; my entire being, bless His holy Name. **JUNE 1**

—Ps 103:1

REFLECTION. As we enjoy this beautiful time of year, we do well to pause to praise and thank God for His wonderful creation. There are many times and places in our universe when we are exposed to spectacular beauty.

As we praise God for this, we wonder what heaven will be like.

PRAYER. *We give You thanks and praise, Almighty God, for the wonders of Your creation. May we always respond to Your generosity by protecting what You have created.*

YOU are the light of the world. A city built upon a mountain cannot be hidden. —Mt 5:14

REFLECTION. When we live out our baptismal promises as followers of Jesus, we light up a darkened world. On our mountain of faith, we become a beam of hope for others who experience the darkness of life without God.

Let prayer feed our light.

PRAYER. *God of wisdom, You invite Your people to be light for others, as was Jesus for us. May we always walk in the way of Gospel light and bring others safely home to You.*

 PAUL remained there in his lodgings for two full years at his own expense. He welcomed all who came to him, and without hindrance he boldly proclaimed the Kingdom of God and taught about the Lord Jesus Christ. —Acts 28:30-31

REFLECTION. As we live out our lives of faith, like Paul, we have the assurance of the Holy Spirit's presence. That is why we can speak about the Lord Jesus Christ, His works and His Word.

We can easily give an account of our beliefs to those who would walk with us.

PRAYER. *God of peace, in a world troubled by upheaval, violence, and disbelief, may we always maintain the fullness of the Spirit through lives free of sin. Keep us in the power of Your abiding presence and grace.*

ALL of them look to You to give them their food at the appropriate time. When You provide it for them, they gather it up; when You open Your hand, they are filled with good things.

JUNE 4

—Ps 104:27-28

REFLECTION. In the Holy Eucharist we receive the Good of all goods. No earthly nourishment can match the wonder of the Body and Blood of Christ. We walk the road to eternal salvation well nourished.

We need not even think of the forbidden fruit of the knowledge of good and evil.

PRAYER. *God, our loving Father, we are filled with joy when we receive the Eucharist. Help us to free ourselves from sin that we may receive the Lord each day.*

JESUS said to them, "Give to Caesar what is due to Caesar, and to God what is due to God."

JUNE 5

—Mk 12:17

REFLECTION. Everything we have belongs to God. So, we are on the right course when we strive to give back everything to God.

While we must fulfill life's necessities, we know our focus on God should be in completing the duties of our state in life.

PRAYER. *God of peace and justice, may we always live for You alone. Help us to avoid the pitfalls and attractions of worldliness and attachment to material things.*

E is not the God of the dead but of the living. You are very badly mistaken. —Mk 12:27

REFLECTION. Our Lord Jesus Christ overcame the sting of death. We rise with Jesus through our baptism and the life-giving Bread of Angels.

In the midst of the most challenging of worldly temptations and confrontation, we stand firm in the joy and knowledge of life that will never end.

PRAYER. *Almighty Father of the universe, we praise and thank You for having saved us from the death of sin. Keep us always in Your grace through the powerful presence of the Holy Spirit.*

 LESSED are all those who fear the Lord and walk in His ways. —Ps 128:1

REFLECTION. As followers of Jesus, we have a great remedy for the ever-present anxiety of our age.

Merely to walk in the ways of the Lord is to achieve the happiness worldly attachments, ways, means, and philosophy cannot provide.

PRAYER. *Lord God, be with us as we live out our lives according to Your Will. May we remain steadfast in our baptismal promises.*

YOU shall love the Lord your God with all your heart, and with all your soul, and with all your mind, and with all your strength. —Mk 12:30

JUNE 8

REFLECTION. In our country's vast highway system, directional signs of the same design and color can lead us across the nation without a hitch.

Jesus' words on how we should love, if followed, will take us to eternal life.

PRAYER. *Ever-loving Father, You show us how to love by giving us Your only Son for our salvation. Let us never fall into the temptation to give up loving others.*

 THEN He called His disciples to Him and said, "Amen, I say to you, this poor widow has given more than all the other contributors to the treasury." —Mk 12:43

JUNE 9

REFLECTION. Jesus had a deep appreciation for the poor and those who struggled with the needs of everyday life. He instructs the disciples that the poorest of the poor are an essential fabric for the followers of Jesus.

What do we think of the poor? What do we do about them?

PRAYER. *God, our Father, You call us Your sons and daughters and ask us to live in charity for and with one another. May we always give that little extra share in helping Your beloved poor.*

AY the God of hope fill you with all joy and peace in believing, so that you may grow rich in hope by the power of the Holy Spirit. —Rom 15:13

JUNE 10

REFLECTION. We recall the Divine indwelling of the Holy Spirit as we move from day to day. Realizing that the Spirit is with us, no matter the challenges of the day or age, we have hope in the salvation promised us.

This should be a tonic for our challenged lives.

PRAYER. *O Most Holy Trinity, as we rejoice in the knowledge of Your great love for us, help us never to forget Your special presence among us at all times.*

 ET those who love the Lord hate evil, for He protects the souls of His faithful ones and rescues them from the hand of the wicked. —Ps 97:10

JUNE 11

REFLECTION. Jesus told Thomas that He was the Way, the Truth, and the Life. With the Lord we strive to always hate the evil of our times.

Walking in the light of the Spirit, we know that nothing can harm us spiritually.

PRAYER. *God of wisdom, You invite us to walk honestly and uprightly on our journey home. May we embrace the Spirit and live lives of virtue in Your presence.*

HOWEVER, it is God Who enables both us and you to stand firm in Christ. He has anointed us and marked us with His seal and given us the Spirit in our hearts. —2 Cor 1:21

JUNE 12

REFLECTION. Like the disciples of old, we are the anointed of the Lord in the modern age.

We carry the message of Jesus Christ, and we do not compromise with this age, individually or as Church.

PRAYER. *God of power and might, we turn to You in time of temptation and need. Do not let us falter as we seek to live a life of goodness and peace.*

BUT thanks be to God, for He brings us to victory in Christ and through us manifests the fragrance of the knowledge of Him throughout the world. —2 Cor 2:14

JUNE 13

REFLECTION. As we live out the Word of God in our ordinary lives, we become an extraordinary people. Others come to know who, what and why we are; and they seek to be with us in body and spirit.

These are the outcomes of living God's Word.

PRAYER. *Almighty God, You call us to be the salt of the earth, a light to lead others back to You. May we persevere in good and never weaken in our task.*

O on your way. Behold, I am sending you out like lambs among wolves.
—Lk 10:3

JUNE 14

REFLECTION. When we walk in the light of Christ, we may be a challenge for others. We gladly accept confrontation and criticism for the Kingdom.

In the workplace and at home, we conduct ourselves as did Christ.

PRAYER. *God of power and might, we gladly walk in the footsteps of Jesus and accept the difficulties we encounter. May we bless with prayer and peace those who oppose us.*

 WILL listen for God's response; surely the Lord will proclaim peace to His people, His Saints, to those who turn to Him with their whole heart.
—Ps 85:9

JUNE 15

REFLECTION. As a people of hope we search our personal lives for peace. We seek to be in God's grace. Then we share our peace on the highway, in the workplace and, above all, in our family relationships.

Stony silence and a refusal to communicate with one another is proof of a lack of peace that flies in the face of God.

PRAYER. *God of peace, we come to You burdened with inner and interpersonal conflicts. May we always imitate You and Your Son, learning to be peace for all people without exception.*

LESS the Lord, O my soul, and do not forget all His benefits. —Ps 103:2

REFLECTION. We lift our minds and hearts in prayer as we recall the many gifts God has given us.

The words of Jesus tell of the goodness of God in our regard. And we are filled with hope over that which is to come.

PRAYER. *Lord of heaven and earth, we praise and thank You for the abundance of Your gifts to Your people. May we always remember to return and give thanks and praise.*

 HE Lord is merciful and gracious, slow to anger and abounding in kindness. —Ps 103:8

REFLECTION. Sometimes it is good to ask ourselves whether we can afford not to be gracious and merciful like our Lord.

If we are holding a grudge, or refusing to speak with someone, we need to overcome our anger and reach out in kindness.

PRAYER. *God of peace and love, we praise You for having forgiven us our sins. Help us to understand the necessity of imitating Your merciful compassion.*

E died for all, so that those who live might no longer live for themselves, but for Him Who for their sakes died and was raised to life. **JUNE 18** —2 Cor 5:15

REFLECTION. Living in and for the Lord Who died to redeem us, makes us partners in His mission on earth. Redemption has been accomplished for all.

In our lives, conformed to Jesus', we promote salvation for others.

PRAYER. *God of wisdom, You call us to share in the work of redemption. Grant us the discipline to walk closely in the mind of Jesus so that we might bring His Good News to those most in need.* _____

N Christ you also heard the message of truth and the Gospel of your salvation, and you came to believe in Him. **JUNE 19** —Eph 1:13

REFLECTION. Like St. Paul, our energy and zeal for spreading the Word of God enable us to stand in for both God the Father and His Son.

To do God's work, bringing salvation news to others, is both a privilege and responsibility. It can easily become a way of life.

PRAYER. *God of the universe, we work to bring the message of Your love to all people. Help us to persevere in doing good and provide good example for all who are open to conversion.*

OU have heard that it was said, "An eye for an eye and a tooth for a tooth." But I say to you: Offer no resistance to someone who is wicked. If someone strikes you on your right cheek, turn and offer him the other cheek as well.

JUNE 20

—Mt 5:38-40

REFLECTION. We hear much about road rage today and its sometimes tragic and deadly consequences.

Jesus' admonition might well be taken as we drive from place to place, giving way and remaining patient to the best of our ability.

PRAYER. *Loving Father, as we move from place to place, help us with Your patience and calm. May we never seek to outdo another in speed and position.*

OU have heard that it was said, "You shall love your neighbor and hate your enemy." But I say to you: Love your enemies and pray for those who persecute you.

JUNE 21

—Mt 5:43-44

REFLECTION. The words of Jesus turn our world upside down. It takes great grace and prayer to refrain from lashing out against those who consider themselves our enemies.

Praying for them is a soothing balm and may lead to reconciliation.

PRAYER. *Loving Father, enable us to be brother and sister to both friend and foe. May we always actively pray for and be kind to those who seemingly hate us.*

BEWARE of performing righteous deeds before others in order to impress them. If you do so, you will receive no reward from your Father in heaven. —Mt 6:1

JUNE 22

REFLECTION. Americans are noted throughout the world for their generosity to those in need. It is good to be of help to those who are in want, but the Lord advises us not to make a show of our charity.

Our hidden poor boxes could well become a quiet destination for us each weekend.

PRAYER. *Heavenly Father, we give You thanks and praise for the many blessings You have given us in this life. Make us aware of those who are more in need than we so that we might tender Your love and care for them.*

 AS a shepherd seeks out his flock when he is among his scattered sheep, so I will seek out My sheep. I will rescue them from wherever they were scattered during the clouds and darkness. —Ezek 34:12

JUNE 23

REFLECTION. We may lose our way in the clouds and darkness of temptation and sin.

But we have the great consolation of knowing that our Good Shepherd will rescue us, whenever we want to be saved.

PRAYER. *God of power and might, look after us as we walk the paths of destruction and death in an unfriendly world. May we never fail to turn to You should we fall into sin.*

93

THUS, God proved His love for us in that while we were still sinners Christ died for us. —Rom 5:8

JUNE 24

REFLECTION. Blood and water flowing from the side of Christ on Calvary is an all-encompassing symbol of God's love for us sinners.

The sign of God's Sacred Heart on fire and crowned with thorns gives us deep insight into the depth of God's love for His people.

PRAYER. *Father of mercy and love, as we recall the heart of Jesus split open for our salvation, may we give ourselves more fully to bringing others to the cooling shade of Your abundant love for all.*

TASTE and see that the Lord is good; blessed is the man who takes refuge in Him. —Ps 34:9

JUNE 25

REFLECTION. We have a standing invitation to go on vacation, even if only for a few minutes.

By recalling God's presence in any way that appeals to us, we settle into quiet prayer for a few moments. Peace and joy enter in where before there were noise and confusion.

PRAYER. *Lord, our God, You call us into the refuge of Your presence. Help us to look forward to spending time with You at many times throughout the day.*

E went down with them and came to Nazareth, and He was obedient to them. His mother pondered all these things in her heart. —Lk 2:51

JUNE 26

REFLECTION. We have been blessed with Jesus and Mary as models of obedience. Mary's yes gave us redemption and salvation.

Jesus' yes to His parents showed us how to obey those whom the Lord has put over us in authority.

PRAYER. *Father of peace and justice, we look to Your Son, Jesus, to show us the way home to You. Nourished for the journey, help us keep our eternal goal ever in mind.*

 RIOR to His coming, John had already proclaimed a baptism of repentance to all the people of Israel. —Acts 13:24

JUNE 27

REFLECTION. As we recall the vocation of John the Baptist, the promises made for us at our baptism could readily be reviewed.

We expressed our beliefs in the teaching of the Church, and promised, through our god-parents, to do all that is necessary to remain in the grace of God.

PRAYER. *Almighty God, through Your Son, Jesus Christ, we have been called to walk in the light of everlasting life. May we never seek the shadows of sin and death.*

HY do you take note of the splinter in your brother's eye but do not notice the wooden plank in your own eye? —Mt 7:3

JUNE 28

REFLECTION. When we converse uncharitably about others, the poison we speak can bring deadly harm to our souls, indeed to our salvation.

Our critical speech can seem so easy and comfortable. Still, it could be our greatest challenge as a disciple of Jesus.

PRAYER. *Father of life, through slander and detraction, we sin against Your love and care for all Your people. May we examine our own hearts before speaking uncharitably.*

HEN Abram said to Lot, "Let there be no strife between you and me, or between your herders and mine, for we are kinsmen." —Gen 13:8

JUNE 29

REFLECTION. God asks us to live in peace with one another. Family strife and bickering should not be accepted among Jesus' followers.

The saying, "Charity begins at home," is not only wise, but also a notion lived that can save us much grief and sin.

PRAYER. *God, our Father, in Your great wisdom You established the family as the bedrock of human society. May we never do anything to bring about disharmony in our families and neighborhoods.*

E on guard against false prophets who come to you disguised in sheep's clothing, but who inwardly are ravenous wolves. **JUNE 30** —Mt 7:15

REFLECTION. Many times, some who would have us live by slogans are really false prophets. "Try it; it won't hurt you." "Just do it this once." "You haven't lived; you better get started." "Everybody else is doing it."

In many instances, these are temptations to sin. Before reacting, it's best to check with Church teaching and God's Word.

PRAYER. *Almighty God, Creator of heaven and earth, watch over us as we make our way through life in a world turned upside down by sin. Keep us safe from the pitfalls of ease, sensuality, and comfort.*

 ROTECT me, O God, for in You I take refuge. I say to the Lord, "You are my Lord; I have no good apart from You." **JULY 1** —Ps 16:1-2

REFLECTION. In times of trouble, stress, disappointment, and upset, we easily turn to the Lord and seek His guidance and counsel.

What a wonderful God we have, always ready to embrace us in our hour of need and be with us in times of joy.

PRAYER. *Gracious and loving God, we praise and thank You for Your great care for Your people. May we always turn to You in our hour of need.*

UNDOUBTEDLY you have heard about my former way of life in Judaism, how I fiercely persecuted the Church of God and tried to destroy it. —Gal 1:13

JULY 2

REFLECTION. We can take heart in Paul's conversion, while, at the same time, we get a glimpse of the mind and heart of God. No matter how we resist, the Lord wants us with Him for all eternity.

So now is the time to give up, give in, and accept God.

PRAYER. *Merciful Father, in our sinfulness we turn to You and beg Your forgiveness. In turn, help us to forgive others whose slights and insults cannot compare to our sins.*

 HE said to them in reply, "Why are you so frightened, O you of little faith?" Then He stood up and rebuked the winds and the sea, and there was a great calm. —Mt 8:26

JULY 3

REFLECTION. In times of war, terror and economic uncertainty, as a people, we can become filled with fears.

In faith we turn to the Lord, knowing that through His great power and growth in our faith and trust in Him, we have every reason to be calm.

PRAYER. *God, our Father You have made Your people the object of Your care and concern. May our trust in You increase each day.*

I N my anguish I cried out; the Lord heard my plea, and I was saved from all my troubles. —Ps 34:7

JULY 4

REFLECTION. The Psalmist reminds us of the necessity of turning to the Lord in prayer every day.

On any given occasion we may feel at peace, yet we must guard against the onset of temptation by raising our minds and hearts to God.

PRAYER. *Loving Father, we come to You burdened with sin and temptation. Open our minds and hearts to Your loving presence in our lives.*

K EEP your tongue from evil and your lips from telling lies. Shun evil and do good; seek peace and pursue it. —Ps 34:14-15

JULY 5

REFLECTION. It is good to remind ourselves that, through our tongues with which we praise God, we can easily destroy another's reputation through slander and detraction.

As Christ's followers, we should strive never to lie and to speak only good of others.

PRAYER. *God of majesty and truth, we seek Your help in taming our tongues. Never let us use your great gift of speech to bring misery and destruction to another.*

OME people then approached Him, carrying a paralyzed man lying on a bed. On perceiving their faith, Jesus said to the man, "Take heart, son. Your sins are forgiven."
—Mt 9:2

JULY 6

REFLECTION. In God's providence, we sometimes encounter folks crippled with sin. In a Christlike way we bring them to the Lord, where their sins will be forgiven, and they will be restored to true health.

Yes, we are called to and can accomplish Jesus' work.

PRAYER. *God of love and mercy, You bid Your people to live according to Your Law. Sometimes, in weakness, we turn away from Your goodness. Grant us the grace to return for forgiveness.*

E will banish the chariot from Ephraim, and horses from Jerusalem; the bow of war will be banished. He will proclaim peace to the nations. His dominion shall be from sea to sea, and from the River to the ends of the earth. —Zec 9:10

JULY 7

REFLECTION. Peace is God's blessing for His people.

While we are in constant warfare with the evil one so that we might remain faithful to our God, we know that, at the end of the struggle, our Promised Land will be one of peace.

PRAYER. *God of love and mercy, hear our prayer as we seek the peace of Your Kingdom. Let us always, with Your grace, fight the wiles of the devil.*

F you do live according to the flesh, you will die. However, if by the Spirit you put to death the deeds of the body, you will live. **JULY 8** —Rom 8:13

REFLECTION. During vacation time when we kick back, temptations of the flesh can join us.

We avoid the death of sins of the flesh by consciously practicing the presence of God and looking to Mary for help in tight situations.

PRAYER. *God, our Father, through the intercession of the Most Blessed Virgin and St. Joseph, keep us pure in mind and heart. May we live so as to be worthy of the Kingdom.*

 OME to Me, all you who are weary and overburdened, and I will give you rest. **JULY 9** —Mt 11:28

REFLECTION. We are bombarded on TV and radio about the need to pause and seek a refreshing break.

As followers of Jesus, we know that turning to God in a few minutes of meditative prayer can easily lift up our spirits and give us the courage and energy to move on with our lives.

PRAYER. *God of love and peace, we come to You in times of stress and overwork. We know that You will refresh us in the wisdom of Your bounty. May we never forget Your blessings to us each hour of the day.*

THE house of Israel trusts in the Lord; He is their help and their shield.

—Ps 115:9

JULY 10

REFLECTION. The great heritage of Christianity is the house of Israel. We inherit their great notion of trust, much exercised by many trials and challenges.

In the Church of Jesus Christ, we place our trust in the Lord during stormy weather both as Church and individuals.

PRAYER. *Lord, our God, we look to You for protection, guidance, and direction in difficult times. We wholeheartedly accept Your promise to be with us till the end. Help us to live this truth.*

JESUS traveled through all the towns and villages, teaching in their synagogues, proclaiming the Good News of the Kingdom, and curing every illness and disease.

—Mt 9:35

JULY 11

REFLECTION. We hear the Word of God and hope that Jesus will visit our village, especially when we are taken with the disease of indifference and neglect.

We know that if we turn to Him or invite Him into our homes, He will cure us. Truly we must want to be healed.

PRAYER. *All-powerful and ever-merciful God, come to the aid of Your people. We are drowning in our neglect of Your Word and Commandments. Help us to respond to Your grace that we might live.*

HOUGH I write for him My many precepts, they are considered as those of a stranger. —Hos 8:12 **JULY 12**

REFLECTION. When we are a stranger to God's Word put into action in our lives, we reap the idolatry of the present moment, the flesh and the profane.

In the shortness of our days, it is important to focus on God's desire to be paramount in our minds and hearts.

PRAYER. *O God, loving Father, open Your arms to receive us back into Your home. Help us to burn away our past indifference and neglect of Your commands.*

 ETURN, O Israel, to the Lord, your God; your guilt caused you to stumble. —Hos 14:2 **JULY 13**

REFLECTION. From the earliest days of God's Covenant with His people, an open invitation to return to the Lord still stands.

When we are haunted with guilt, we need look no further than the Spirit dwelling within us. We can focus and listen for God's comforting message.

PRAYER. *Heavenly Father, we come to You burdened with the guilt of our sins and transgressions. Help us to discover wisdom and peace of mind in Your Law.*

AM sending you out like sheep among wolves. Therefore, be as cunning as serpents and yet as innocent as doves.

—Mt 10:16

REFLECTION. Jesus' admonition to His disciples serves us well over two thousand years later.

As we progress in our spiritual lives, each day we may be confronted with new, more cleverly disguised temptations to faith and law. We need to take care so as not to be cornered.

PRAYER. *God, our Father, with courage and grace we live each day that we might be pleasing to You. Shelter us from worldly yet attractive ways that lead only to darkness.*

 OR I have come to set a man against his father, a daughter against her mother, and a daughter-in-law against her mother-in-law; and one's enemies will be the members of his own household.

—Mt 10:35-36

REFLECTION. With interpersonal relationships even within one's family, differences over hearing and accepting the Word of God can be cause for much pain and travail.

We cannot allow this to upset us; hence we remain faithful to the Lord.

PRAYER. *God of wisdom, help us to strengthen family bonds by remaining faithful to Your Word and the teachings of the Church. May our family relationships be based firmly in the love You proclaim.*

EVELOP a plan, but it shall be **JULY 16** thwarted; make a proposal, and it shall not stand, for God is with us.

—Isa 8:10

REFLECTION. The prophet's warning to God's enemies is a source of wisdom for our times.

No matter what forces attack God's people or His Church, God remains with us and our enemies' plans will come to naught. Sometimes they seem to have the upper hand, but their plans are doomed.

PRAYER. *Almighty God, we give You thanks and praise for Your presence among us. May we go forward without fear to meet the challenges of our day.*

 AVE we not all one Father? Did not one **JULY 17** God create us? Why then do we break faith with one another, violating the covenant of our ancestors?

—Mal 2:10

REFLECTION. Maintaining our strong faith becomes the glue of modern society.

In the midst of war and violence throughout the world, we seek to live, as in our Father's house, through gentleness, compassion, and forgiveness.

PRAYER. *Heavenly Father, King of peace, help us to walk together in this life so that, in honoring Your plan for Your people, we may come to the Kingdom You have so generously prepared for us.*

T that time, Jesus said, "I thank You, Father, Lord of heaven and earth, because You have hidden these things from the wise and the learned and have revealed them to children."

JULY 18

—Mt 11:25

REFLECTION. Here we have a valuable insight into the mind of Jesus.

Frustrated with the wise and learned who mishandled His teachings, Jesus acknowledges folks of simple faith who accepted His Word outright.

PRAYER. *Loving Father, You sent Your Son, Jesus, to save us from our pride and open our minds and hearts to Your great love. May we respond to Your love with prayer and praise.*

HE way of the righteous is straight; You smooth the way of the righteous.

JULY 19

—Isa 26:7

REFLECTION. One of the missing elements in our society today is a pervasive sense of justice. Problems of inequity from an individual viewpoint may just seem too challenging.

Still, we must use our God-given talents to raise our voices and work to the best of our ability to see that justice prevails.

PRAYER. *Just Father, give us the courage to seek justice for all Your people. May we always suppress negative feelings surfaced due to individual differences.*

HE Lord looked down from His sanctuary on high and gazed on the earth from heaven, to hear the sighs of the prisoners and to set free those under sentence of death. —Ps 102:20-21

JULY 20

REFLECTION. The Psalmist praises God for hearing the cry of the poor.

How do we allow the Lord's interest and concern for the poor to enter into our lives? Vacation time might be a good time to share our joy with the poor.

PRAYER. *God of endless ages, Father of all goodness, help us live Your concern for the poor. May we be Your hands in lifting up our brothers and sisters in need.*

EHOLD, My Servant, Whom I have chosen, My Beloved in Whom I delight. I will place My Spirit upon Him, and He will proclaim justice to the Gentiles. —Mt 12:18

JULY 21

REFLECTION. The Lord Who was sent to redeem us, Whose message was to go out to the entire world, was the beloved of the Father.

Jesus, having returned to His Father, invites us to proclaim justice to all peoples. We begin by living justice within our families.

PRAYER. *Father of light, unchanging God, may we carry Your torch of justice in a darkening and selfish world. Help us to be unrelenting in our pursuit of truth and justice.*

OU display Your strength when people doubt the absolute degree of Your power, and You rebuke any insolence shown by those who are aware of Your might. —Wis 12:17

REFLECTION. As we live our faith each day, circumstances that arise, calling for word or action in defense of the Faith, can be done with courage and conviction.

When we find ourselves in the midst of slanderous talk, we should withdraw.

PRAYER. *Father of light, show us the way to defend the ramparts of Faith. Give us the courage to speak out when required. May our words and actions imitate those of Jesus.*

 ET them both grow together until harvest. At harvest time, I will tell the reapers, "Collect the weeds first and tie them in bundles to be burned. Then gather the wheat into my barn." —Mt 13:30

REFLECTION. The Lord allows the good and bad to live together on earth. What can appear to be a sense of looseness will be corrected at the end.

Hence, there is the need for constant vigil, prayer, and examination of conscience each day.

PRAYER. *God of wisdom, keep us from adopting the attitude of "all is well with the world." May we always be aware of our destination and take the means to arrive in Your love.*

E who treats his father badly, or chases away his mother is worthless and shameful.　—Prov 19:26

REFLECTION. We live in an age of instant gratification as god. Moreover, our elderly population expands.

To disgrace one's parents is not only disreputable but also is seriously sinful in God's eyes.

PRAYER. *Father of our Lord, Jesus Christ, You sent Your Son to teach us how to live and die. His life was one of great respect and care for His parents. May we always follow His example.*

 MY people, what have I done to you? In what way have I wearied you? Answer Me!　—Mic 6:3

REFLECTION. Micah reminded the Israelites of God's hurt because of their turning away from Him.

In time of temptation, it is good to recall that our sinful actions offend the God of love, the One Who loves us most of all in this world and the next.

PRAYER. *God of all compassion, Father of all goodness, grant us the wisdom to know Your great love for us. May we never stray from Your care.*

ARY Magdalene then went and announced to the disciples, "I have seen the Lord," and repeated what He had said to her. —Jn 20:18

REFLECTION. It is good for us to be aware of the human intervention of Jesus following His Resurrection.

He stayed on earth for a time to prepare us for the challenges of life. Yet, He shared His Resurrection in a simple and understandable way.

PRAYER. *Jesus, our Lord, You gave humans Your assurances of Your Resurrection. We rejoice in the knowledge that the death of sin is overcome. May we live that truth to the best of our ability.*

OU forgave the iniquity of Your people; You canceled all their sins. —Ps 85:3

REFLECTION. What a wonderful world we wake up to every day, knowing that our sins have been completely forgiven.

We face another opportunity to strive, to the best of our ability, to avoid sin each day.

PRAYER. *Almighty God, Father of light, we beg You to enlighten us in times of temptation. May the Eucharist we receive help nourish us on the way home to Your Kingdom.*

OR in our lives we are constantly being given up to death for Jesus' sake, so that the life of Jesus may be revealed in our mortal flesh. **JULY 28** —2 Cor 4:11

REFLECTION. Sometimes it may seem as though we are on our own when it comes to challenges to our beliefs. Folks tell us that we are going the wrong way, or we are mixed up.

Yet, we know that daily mortification is the spice of life for Jesus' followers.

PRAYER. *Lord of mercy, while we walk in the valley of tears, we are not without hope and light. May we always take the means necessary to avoid the darkness of sin.*

 IRD your loins; stand up and tell them everything that I command you. Do not be broken before them, or I will break you before them. **JULY 29** —Jer 1:17

REFLECTION. God's promise to be with His people during challenging times serves us well today. We believe what we believe, and legal or illegal hurdles cannot stop us from living our beliefs.

We may be pressed, but never broken.

PRAYER. *All-powerful Father, we live in the light of Your Word, though the powers of darkness would try to overcome us. Help Your people of faith to adhere to You and live Your Word with courage.*

I F you do not listen, I will weep in secret for your pride; my eyes will flood with tears for the Lord's flock has been led away captive. **JULY 30**

—Jer 13:17

REFLECTION. Just as Jeremiah admonished his people, we need to admonish ourselves.

We tell ourselves to stay away from the exile of computer pornography, immodesty of the eyes, and setting hopes on things we do not need.

PRAYER. *Father of our Lord, Jesus Christ, watch over us, we beg You, as the darkness of sin and temptation is so much a part of this world. May we turn to You in prayer in these times of strife.* _____

A T the Name of Jesus every knee should bend of those in heaven and on earth and under the earth, and every tongue should proclaim to the glory of God the Father: Jesus Christ is Lord. **JULY 31**

—Phil 2:10-11

REFLECTION. All God's creation gives Him honor and glory. He created us in His image and likeness; thus we are called to an active glorification of the Lord in all that we think, say or do.

We are blessed with a precious and privileged intimacy with God.

PRAYER. *Heavenly Father, You have gifted Your people with Your image and likeness. May we praise You as we await the Second Coming of Jesus. Help us to reflect Your goodness in our abiding respect for one another.*

AFTERWARD, all the Israelites came closer, and he gave them all the commands the Lord had told him on Mount Sinai. —Ex 34:32

REFLECTION. Moses was a mediator between God and His people. Today, Jesus enjoins on us all that He preached during His public life.

This can be for us, when observed, a way of life that leads to eternal joy.

PRAYER. *Father in heaven, Creator of all, in Your wisdom You have sent us an invitation to eternal life through Moses and Jesus. May we always accept Your Word and live with You forever.*

 THE Kingdom of Heaven is like treasure buried in a field, which a man found and buried again. Then in his joy he went off and sold everything he had and bought that field. —Mt 13:44

REFLECTION. Following our conversion, we realize that we have the greatest of all treasures.

In this knowledge, we give away all circumstances and places that would lead us into sin and cause us to lose our great gift, our supernatural discovery of a life that will never end.

PRAYER. *Father of light, we look to You to safeguard our call to holiness. May we always live in such a way that we will please You in accomplishing Your Will.*

EXALT the Lord, our God, and worship at His holy mountain, for the Lord, our God, is holy. —Ps 99:9

REFLECTION. What a great blessing for us today to go into the presence of the essence of holiness when we visit our Lord in His tabernacles.

In our striving to be holy, what better way than going into the presence of the Holy of holies, a veritable freewill prisoner in our churches.

PRAYER. *All-powerful and ever-living God, Your Son dwells with us in the Most Blessed Sacrament. May we never forget Your wonderful Gift, and seek out the living Jesus with profound adoration and respect.*

 YOU may work for six days; but the seventh day is a day of complete rest, a day for sacred assembly; you shall do no work. It is a sabbath to the Lord wherever you live. —Lev 23:3

REFLECTION. We gift ourselves by embracing God's Will in our regard. The Lord wants us to turn to Him in a special way on His day, while, at the same time, He wants us to relax and reinvigorate ourselves.

Avoiding our profession or job once a week makes good sense.

PRAYER. *God of mercy and consolation, we seek to do Your Will in all things. May we draw closer to You as we rest from our labors.*

E came to His hometown, and He began to teach the people in the synagogue. They were astonished and wondered, "Where did this man get such wisdom and these mighty deeds?" —Mt 13:54

REFLECTION. Pope John XXIII used to look at the crucifix and say, "They did it to Him; they'll do it to me." It is a good philosophy by which to live.

CCD teachers, adult religious education leaders, lectors, and other volunteers sometimes get the same treatment as Jesus in His hometown. As such, it is our cross to bear.

PRAYER. *God of endless ages, Father, when we answer Your call to work in Your vineyard, some nearest to us can be a challenge. May we always respond with faith and humility to their concerns.*

 GOD, be gracious to us and bless us and let Your face shine upon us.
—Ps 67:2

REFLECTION. In all things we strive to turn toward God. We face the great light of His wisdom, peace, patience, joy and love for us.

We allow ourselves to be nurtured by the Divinity, in preparation for that great day of His coming.

PRAYER. *Father of light, unchanging God, show us the way to Your Kingdom. May we always follow the teachings of Your Son, Jesus, that we might live with You, Jesus and His mother forever.*

HEN a voice came out of the cloud, saying, "This is My Son, My Chosen One. Listen to Him." —Lk 9:35

REFLECTION. The chosen Son of the Father asks us, through Baptism and Confirmation, to become His chosen people. The ancient mandate remains. We listen to the Son of God. In so doing, we cannot go wrong in our lives.

For the worldly we may be different; indeed, we are.

PRAYER. *Father of our Lord Jesus Christ, You have invited us to walk in the footsteps of Your Son. May we always abide by Your commands and live Your Will to the best of our ability.* ⎯⎯⎯⎯⎯⎯

S I looked, thrones were set in place, and the Ancient of Days took His seat. His clothing was as white as snow; the hair of His head was white like wool. His throne was flaming with fire, and its wheels were all ablaze.

—Dan 7:9

REFLECTION. These words give insight into the Kingdom from which the Son of Man came to save us. It stands in vivid contrast to any notion of flames that burn, a deep pit and worms that never die.

Our spirits are lifted toward a Father of light, peace, and compassion.

PRAYER. *Almighty God and Father of light, come to our aid in the valley of temptation and death. May we always carry Your words in our minds and hearts that we may come to know the light.*

HE heavens proclaim His righteousness, and all the nations behold His glory. —Ps 97:6

AUG. 9

REFLECTION. As God's loving Son, Jesus is Lord of heaven and earth. As the Son of Justice itself, followers of Jesus are called to seek justice for all people.

We stand with the poor and foster the cause of the unborn and sick elderly.

PRAYER. *God of all compassion, Father of all goodness, we seek justice for all Your people. May we always follow Your Son, Jesus, in looking with care and concern on all, especially the most rejected.*

 HEY told Moses: "We went into the land to which you sent us. It does indeed flow with milk and honey, this is the fruit of the land." —Num 13:27

AUG. 10

REFLECTION. At times, we have to rise above the fray and confusion that characterize our day. We confirm our belief that the Lord God will remain true to His promises.

We will indeed live in the land of the living.

PRAYER. *Father in heaven, we turn to You with hope in Your promise to make us heirs of Your Kingdom. Help us to live that hope in such a way that others will want to be with us.*

FTER He sent them away, He went by Himself up on the mountain to pray. When evening came, He was there alone. —Mt 14:23

REFLECTION. Jesus gives us the lessons in life that will serve us in good stead.

To become more effective followers of the Lord, prayer has to be part of our very being. Spending a few minutes with the Lord before we sleep is most rewarding.

PRAYER. *Father of our Lord, Jesus Christ, we praise You for the great gift of salvation given us through Your Son. May we, like Him, remain faithful to You in mind and spirit all the days of our life.*

 UT the Lord said to Moses and Aaron, "Because you did not believe I would proclaim My holiness before the Israelites, you shall not lead this community into the land I am giving them." —Num 20:12

REFLECTION. As we embrace the teachings of the Lord, we take great care not to give bad example to anyone, especially the little ones.

Our gift of faith is great, but we are called to live up to it responsibly.

PRAYER. *God, Father of our Savior, You call us to holiness of life as a prelude to the everlasting joy of heaven. Help us to live our lives in such a way that others will see the light.*

OME forth! Let us bow down to worship Him; let us kneel before the Lord, our Maker. For He is our God, and we are the people He shepherds, the flock He protects. —Ps 95:6-7

REFLECTION. Through His Apostles, Jesus established the Church to lead us home to everlasting life.

How appropriate to pause many times throughout the day to praise and thank God for His goodness.

PRAYER. *All-powerful Father, we praise and thank You for Your great goodness in preparing a place for us in Your Kingdom. May we always be worthy of Your great love and compassion for us.*

 ROM then onward Jesus made it clear to His disciples that He must go to Jerusalem and endure great suffering at the hands of the elders, the chief priests, and the scribes, and be put to death, and be raised on the third day. —Mt 16:21

REFLECTION. In Jesus' instruction to His disciples, we come to a full understanding of the necessity of the Cross in our daily lives.

With the same simple reality manifested by Jesus, we follow Him in embracing our crosses.

PRAYER. *God of love and mercy, Your Son, Jesus Christ, suffered and died that we might be forgiven our sins against You. Help us to embrace crosses and contradictions as faithfully as did the Son of Man.*

ELIZABETH was filled with the Holy Spirit, and she exclaimed with a loud cry, "Blessed are you among women, and blessed is the fruit of your womb." **AUG. 15**

—Lk 1:41-42

REFLECTION. By simply accepting her role as mother of the Messiah, Mary is exalted on high.

We share Mary's role by allowing God's Word to grow within us, thereby enabling us to give birth to the Good News of salvation.

PRAYER. *All-powerful and ever-living God, You accomplished the salvation of the world through Mary's simple fiat. May we, like Mary, be ever ready to accept Your call to discipleship.*

WHEN the soles of the feet of the priests bearing the ark of the Lord, the Lord of all the earth, touch the waters of the Jordan, the waters will be stopped and shall stand in one mass. **AUG. 16**

—Jos 3:13

REFLECTION. True to His promise, God takes good care of His people, even to the point of performing a miracle.

Jesus is our Lord, quietly awaiting us in the modern ark of our tabernacles. The miracle of His Real Presence is ours in a very special way.

PRAYER. *Jesus, our Lord, You are present with us in our churches throughout the world. May we strive to watch and pray in Your Real Presence as often as possible.*

TREMBLE, O earth, at the presence of the **AUG.** Lord, at the presence of the God of Jacob, Who turns the rock into a pool of water, and flint into a flowing spring. **17**
—Ps 114:7-8

REFLECTION. Our God is so good and loving that, even when we enter into the Holy of holies, it is by gracious invitation.

With joy and without fear we come into God's Real Presence in the Blessed Sacrament.

PRAYER. *All-powerful Father, we come into Your presence with peace and joy. Keep us always in Your care. and never let us stray from the path to eternal life.*

THE people answered, "Far be it from **AUG.** us to desert the Lord and serve other gods." **18**
—Jos 24:16

REFLECTION. Each day we are tested by a variety of gods who would dissuade us from our goal. Greed, anger, selfishness, slander, backbiting, impatience and instant gratification seek our obedience and adoration.

We look to the resolve of our ancestors and hold fast to it.

PRAYER. *God, our Father, we acknowledge You as the one true God. You watch over us and guide Your people in good times and bad. May we always seek Your help when tempted.*

THEN people brought children to Him so that He might lay His hands on them and pray. The disciples rebuked them, but Jesus said, "Let the little children come to Me, and do not hinder them. For it is to such as these that the Kingdom of Heaven belongs." —Mt 19:13-14

AUG.

19

REFLECTION. We recall the importance of good example, especially in the presence of children. Parents and others responsible for the spiritual welfare of children need to take their responsibility seriously.

In our relationships with children, we must avoid any cause for rebuke.

PRAYER. *Almighty God and Father of light, through Jesus' words You give us insight into the requirements for heaven. May we always guard our children from evil and imitate their love and simplicity.*

I AM moved with compassion for these people, because they have been with Me now for three days and have had nothing to eat. —Mk 8:2

AUG.

20

REFLECTION. Jesus' concern for those who followed and listened to Him can be a great source of consolation.

Despite life's challenges, the Lord, we are assured, will take care of our needs, both physical and spiritual.

PRAYER. *Lord, our God, we turn to You in all our needs. We praise and thank You for giving us hope to sustain us each day as we move closer to You.*

O one after lighting a lamp covers it with a pot or places it under a bed. Rather he places it on a lampstand so that those who enter may see the light. —Lk 8:16

REFLECTION. Having been blessed with God's Word and a great gift of faith, we are called to be stand-up followers of Christ. Like Jesus, we must stay the course in face of opposition, criticism, and scandal.

Our light is Christ's light and we need to let it shine at all times.

PRAYER. *God of mercy and consolation, may we share Your forgiveness and ease the pain, frustration, and fear of all people of goodwill. Let our conduct light their way to salvation.*

 HEN the Angel said to her, "Do not be afraid, Mary, for you have found favor with God. Behold, you will conceive in your womb and bear a Son, and you will name Him Jesus." —Lk 1:30-31

REFLECTION. Like Mary, we have found favor with God. And we discover it in the Person of Jesus, presented to her brothers and sisters by Mary.

We enhance our relationship with Jesus through Mary.

PRAYER. *Lord, our God, we seek to do Your Will in all things. Strengthened by Mary's good example, we strive to grow in the way of Jesus through His Word.*

E asked You for life, and You gave it to him, length of days forever and ever. **AUG. 23** —Ps 21:5

REFLECTION. God's love for us far exceeds any sense of human justice that we can muster. Still, we must strive to be just in all actions and thoughts.

As people of justice, we may capture the minds and hearts of others.

PRAYER. *God of love and mercy, with confidence we bring Your wisdom, light, and justice to the world. Where we experience rejection, may we call to mind Your Son's death on the Cross.* —————————

 N that day, a great trumpet will sound, and those lost in the land of Assyria and those exiled to the land of Egypt will come and worship the Lord on the holy mountain, in Jerusalem. **AUG. 24** —Isa 27:13

REFLECTION. Isaiah's words, spoken for a comparatively much smaller world than ours is today, preached the authenticity of God's promise to His people.

Sometimes, our salvation may seem almost impossible, but in faith we persevere to the end.

PRAYER. *Father, all-powerful God, Creator of the universe, we bless and praise Your Name for Your great goodness in bringing us to the altar of salvation. May our lives be worthy of Your great gift.*

H E carried me away in the spirit to the top of a very high mountain and showed me the holy city Jerusalem coming down out of heaven from God. It possessed the glory of God and had the radiance of some priceless jewel, like jasper, clear as crystal. **AUG. 25** —Rev 21:10-11

REFLECTION. It is good for us to have a glimpse of the Kingdom, even if mere words can't in any way come near to describing its reality.

The picture absorbed in mind and heart can be a force for persevering in good.

PRAYER. *God of mercy and consolation, in striving for the Kingdom, You bless us with inspired words that help us to understand, if only in a finite way, Your great love and generosity for Your people.*

N ATHANAEL said to him, "Can anything good come from Nazareth?" Philip replied, "Come and see." **AUG. 26** —Jn 1:46

REFLECTION. In our age of diversity, we see how foolish we can be if we judge others by external characteristics.

At the same time, we recall the universality of the Church and remember that people of all sizes, shapes, and colors share with us the Body and Blood of Christ.

PRAYER. *God of power and life, we ask a share in Your creative wisdom that we might set aside any prejudices we carry in our hearts. May we always strive to live in peace with all peoples.*

THEY were satisfied; when satisfied their hearts grew proud; they then forgot Me. —Hos 13:6

AUG. 27

REFLECTION. Our land, in comparison to others, is almost like the Promised Land.

Our high standard of living and the multiple natural resources with which we are blessed might convince us that, having gorged ourselves on the blessings of this world, we may forget God and the next.

PRAYER. *Almighty God, Father of light, help us to avoid the sin of attachment to material things. May we always acknowledge You as the source of all our blessings.*

 ALL those who exalt themselves will be humbled, and all those who humble themselves will be exalted. —Mt 23:12

AUG. 28

REFLECTION. One of Jesus' titles was Servant. He came to save us, not as a great potentate, but as One Who exhorts us to wash one another's feet.

A life of humility and simplicity is worth the price of admission into the Kingdom.

PRAYER. *All-powerful and unseen God, You sent Your only Son to save us from our sins. Born into poverty, hounded by political leaders, He accepted all for us. May we always imitate His living.*

126

AM coming to gather the nations of every language. They shall come and see My glory.
—Isa 66:18

AUG. 29

REFLECTION. As a people we share with the remainder of the world our invitation to the Kingdom.

Realizing that no one is excluded from the Kingdom, we seek better relations with all peoples, both at home and abroad.

PRAYER. *Father of the universe, despite our physical and religious differences, help us to remain in Your grace. May we be open to all peoples of good faith.*

 OU have forgotten the exhortation that addresses you as children: "My son, do not scorn the discipline of the Lord or lose heart when you are punished by Him."
—Heb 12:5

AUG. 30

REFLECTION. Humanly speaking, correction is difficult to accept.

Nonetheless, when the Lord disciplines us, we need to understand how great a blessing that can be. Our willingness to accept His directives can save us forever.

PRAYER. *Loving Father, as You watch over us and direct us in Your ways, help us to understand the depth of Your love for Your people. May we always respond to Your loving corrections.*

F you, then, despite your evil nature, know how to give good gifts to your children, how much more will the heavenly Father give the Holy Spirit to those who ask Him!

AUG. 31

—Lk 11:13

REFLECTION. Jesus' adversaries attacked Him as a hypocrite.

Working with the Lord's gifts and the talents He bestows, we strive to imitate His design for His people. Our goodness and conformity to God's Will must be evident, even without words.

PRAYER. *Lord of heaven and earth, help us to bring understanding to those who are seeking the truth. May Your words console them and bring them light.*

 UT if salt loses its taste, what can be done to make it salty once again?

SEPT. 1

—Mt 5:13

REFLECTION. One of the biggest complaints we hear from our friends concerns salt. When the doctor orders us off salt, our food becomes bland.

Jesus used a very practical example to show how dull our relationship can be with Him when we begin to let our spiritual lives lag. Reading Scripture and spiritual books helps us to remedy this situation.

PRAYER. *God, our Father, Your Word can fire us up with zeal and enthusiasm for the Kingdom. Help us to never relax our efforts to become more like You.*

HY do you entertain such thoughts in your hearts?

—Mk 2:8

SEPT.

2

REFLECTION. Sometimes we let our minds idle. That is when thoughts most foreign to our spiritual welfare seep in and cause an immense amount of destruction.

Through ejaculatory prayer, we can easily overcome these kinds of distractions. Jesus, Mary, and Joseph love for us to invoke their names.

PRAYER. *Father in heaven, Creator of all, our very surroundings announce the beauty of Your abiding love for us. May we always think only of the good things in life that You give us.*

 E do not wish you to be uncertain, brethren, about those who have fallen asleep. You should not grieve as do those who have no hope. —1 Thes 4:13

SEPT.

3

REFLECTION. Paul assures the church of Thessalonica that the dead will share in the reign of the Lord when He comes. This measure of hope is good for all of us today.

Christ promised to go back to the Father to prepare a place for each of us. Our awareness of the Lord's promise can soften our leaving loved ones behind.

PRAYER. *Eternal Father, You bid us come to You and remain with You forever. Help us to accept Your Will in our regard, and keep us in Your love and grace, especially in times of temptation.*

FOR you yourselves are fully aware that the Day of the Lord will come like a thief in the night. —1 Thes 5:2

REFLECTION. Our morning and evening prayers alert us to the coming of the Lord. As we begin and end each day, we offer all our works, trials, temptations and joys to the Lord.

This way we will attempt to make ourselves ready for the Lord's coming.

PRAYER. *God, our Father, through the intercession of St. Joseph, we ask to be spared a sudden and unprovided death. May we always walk in the light of Jesus, Mary, and Joseph.*

COULD you not keep watch with Me just one hour? —Mt 26:40

REFLECTION. Jesus' words to His disciples in the garden remind us of not only the need, but also the blessing of keeping watch with the Lord.

If our duties prevent our entering a church, we can use a quiet place at home or outside where we encounter the Lord and simply remain in His presence.

PRAYER. *Lord of mercy, You are available to us in so many ways and give us opportunities to rest in Your presence. Help us to come to You every day and drink in Your loving kindness.*

THE people were all amazed, and they said to one another: "What is this teaching! For with authority and power He gives commands to unclean spirits, and they come forth." —Lk 4:36

REFLECTION. In reading and meditating on Scripture, we open ourselves to the great power of God. In the face of every temptation and confrontation, God's Word serves us well.

Reading and living a small portion of the Bible each day is well worthwhile for the follower of Jesus.

PRAYER. *Father of light, unchanging God, help us to hear Your message and to live it to the best of our ability. May we always rejoice in Your plan for us.*

HE is the Head of the Body, that is, the Church. He is the Beginning, the First-born from the dead, so that in every way He should be supreme.

—Col 1:18-19

REFLECTION. It is incumbent upon us to proclaim the primacy of Christ. In all matters pertaining to our personal lives and our community actions in the Church, Christ holds first place.

Inwardly, when we hold Christ above all, we follow Him closely without care or concern.

PRAYER. *Father of our Lord, Jesus Christ, we give You thanks and praise for having sent Your Son to redeem us. May we always live Jesus' Word and follow His example.*

BEHOLD, the virgin shall conceive and give birth to a Son, and they shall name Him Emmanuel, a name that means "God is with us." —Mt 1:23

REFLECTION. Mary, the mother of Jesus, was born into a home of great love and grinding poverty. The One to Whom she was to give birth, and Who would save the world from sin was likewise born into great poverty.

If poverty was good enough for Jesus and Mary, why not for us?

PRAYER. *Father in heaven, You chose a humble servant girl to become the mother of Your Son. May we always reach out to the poor with great respect and generosity.*

HAVE all these evildoers no understanding? They devour My people as they eat bread, and they never call upon the Lord. But later they will be filled with terror, for God is on the side of the righteous. —Ps 14:4-5

REFLECTION. Even in the land of plenty, we can easily overlook the needs of the poor. With so many material conveniences in abundance, we may easily lose sight of our fundamental option for the poor.

The poor box in church should be visited, not ignored.

PRAYER. *Eternal Father, in the lives of Jesus, Mary, and Joseph, we see how readily they embraced the poverty of their day. May we learn from their example and be happy to share our surplus with the poor.*

WITH difficulty do we assess what is on earth, and that which is within our reach we discover only after arduous labor; who then can seek out the things of heaven? **SEPT. 10** —Wis 9:16

REFLECTION. It is really very difficult to know or understand the ways of the Lord. We look upon the wonders of the world, and sometimes they become idols for us.

It is better for us to set aside all worldly things, and follow Jesus without reservation.

PRAYER. *God of wisdom and glory, look upon Your people with compassion. Help us to overcome our weakness and seek only the good that rests with You.*

THE Lord is my light and my salvation; whom should I fear? The Lord is the stronghold of my life; of whom should I be afraid? **SEPT. 11** —Ps 27:1

REFLECTION. The presence of terrorists in our midst has led to staggering statistics of fear among people of all ages.

Like the Israelites of old, we proclaim our hope in the Lord for both safety and refuge and we live calmly in His presence.

PRAYER. *God of mercy and consolation, we turn to You in times of chaos and destruction. May our hope and confidence in You be for others a source of comfort and assurance.*

THE compassion of human beings is for their neighbors, but the compassion of the Lord extends to everyone. He rebukes, trains, and teaches them, . . . as a shepherd does his flock. —Sir 18:12-13

REFLECTION. Both charity and mercy begin at home. Within our families, we look to the mercy of God, the Father, and His Son, Jesus, as exemplars of how families should treat one another.

It is very easy to excuse ourselves from this design, but that can jeopardize our eternal salvation.

PRAYER. *God of love and mercy, we call out to You in our troubled family relationships. Help us to avoid anger and that penetrating silence that can destroy love.*

HOW many loaves do you have?

—Mk 6:38

REFLECTION. Those who followed Jesus during His public life heard the Word, the Bread of eternal Life. The loaves were nourishment for human beings. Still, Jesus knew that He would multiply the loaves to feed the crowds.

Today, He continues to feed us with the Bread of Life in the Eucharist.

PRAYER. *Heavenly Father, we rejoice in the living presence of Your Son, Jesus, in tabernacles throughout the world. Help us deepen our faith in Your generous gift of Eucharist through prayerful reception and study.*

O not be governed by your passions but keep your desires in check. **SEPT.**

—Sir 18:30 **14**

REFLECTION. Advances in communication have exploded in our society. At the same time, evil forces use technological advances to destroy the beauty and purity of interpersonal relations.

When we are tempted by sexual innuendo, whispering the name of Jesus will save us.

PRAYER. *Father of creation, the powers of Satan would corrupt the beauty of Your creation, and use us as his instruments. May we always avoid dangerous occasions and control our evil desires through prayer and fasting.*

———————

 ATHER, He emptied Himself, taking the form of a slave, being born in human likeness. Being found in appearance as a man, He humbled Himself, and became obedient to death, even death on a Cross. **SEPT.** **15**

—Phil 2:7-8

REFLECTION. Every facet of Jesus' life was accomplished in the shadow of the Cross. Despised, rejected, ridiculed—even in the face of good works—Jesus did not hesitate to mount the Cross as a criminal so that we might live forever.

What great love Jesus has for us!

PRAYER. *Jesus, our Lord, You willingly concluded Your life with an excruciating Crucifixion. May we always respond to Your love by striving never to sin or dishonor Your Name.*

E Who lives forever is the Creator of the entire universe. The Lord alone is just. —Sir 18:1

REFLECTION. We need to take time every once in awhile to recall that material things are simply that, things. The one great truth we have is the awareness that the Lord is just.

And we will not find justice in this world aside from Jesus.

PRAYER. *Heavenly Father, Source of all peace and justice, grant us the true wisdom to understand that all things begin and end with You. May we always seek only Your justice.*

 S anything brighter than the sun? Yet it is subject to eclipse. Thus flesh and blood devise evil plans. —Sir 17:26

REFLECTION. Jesus assures us that the brilliance of His children who care for and use their bodies only according to God's Law is far more brilliant than the sun.

It is a light that will shine forever, and one that can change the world.

PRAYER. *Almighty Father and God of light, through purity of mind, heart and body, may we rejoice in the light of Christ. Help us to be raised in union with Jesus that others may be drawn to Your salvation.*

O you not realize that whatever goes into a person from outside cannot defile him, since it enters not into the heart but into the stomach and is discharged into the sewer? —Mk 7:18-19

SEPT. 18

REFLECTION. Here Jesus gives us our passport into the territory of the evil one. Armed with sacramental grace, we may take God's Word into the most despicable places, embracing the foulest communities.

Nothing can hurt us there, and others, by God's grace, may see the light.

PRAYER. *Father, all-powerful God, You give us both hope and protection as we bring the Good News of salvation to those who have fallen into the snares of the devil. Let us never forget Your presence with us at all times.*

 O you still not understand? —Mk 8:21

SEPT. 19

REFLECTION. It is good to examine our actions in light of Who it was that saved us, what He did for us, and perhaps, most importantly, what He said to us.

A daily, evening examination of conscience, mirrored in the light of the Lord's teachings, can help us grow in God's love.

PRAYER. *God of power and mercy, as we follow Jesus in all things, keep us on the straight and narrow. Be with us as we cleanse our conscience at the end of each day.*

WILL rejoice in Jerusalem and delight in My people. No more shall the sound of weeping or the sound of cries be heard there. —Isa 65:19

REFLECTION. We are invited to share in the delights of the new Jerusalem. Jesus has opened the way for us. The admission price are charity, peace, and justice lived today in imitation of Jesus.

Truly, our lives will become a beacon for others to follow.

PRAYER. *God of mercy and consolation, You bring joy and peace to Your people as we repent of our sins. May we always seek Your truth and goodness in all things.*

 UT for that very reason I was treated mercifully, so that in me Jesus Christ might exhibit His inexhaustible patience, making me an example for those who would come to believe in Him for eternal life.

—1 Tim 1:16

REFLECTION. Paul speaks for all of us as sinners. With Paul, we proclaim that each is the foremost of offenders.

Still, having been assured of forgiveness and glory, we strive to become examples to the degree that others will follow enthusiastically.

PRAYER. *Merciful Father, we praise and glorify Your Name for Your mercy in washing away our sins. May we live virtuous lives and sanctify Your Church in its mission.*

DESIRE, then, that in every place the men should pray, lifting up their hands reverently in prayer without anger or argument.
—1 Tim 2:8

SEPT. 22

REFLECTION. Paul's letters to the Gentiles offer directions on how converts to Christianity should act. The community should be an oasis of prayer, where rancor and disagreement have no place.

When we pray in the community of the Church, we avail ourselves of needed peace.

PRAYER. *O God of all the nations, we come to You seeking refuge from the deluge of temptation in our lives. Refresh us with Your presence, understanding, and compassion.*

 HOSE on rock are the ones who, when they hear the Word, receive it with joy. But these have no root; they believe for a short while, but in time of trial they fall away.
—Lk 8:13

SEPT. 23

REFLECTION. Every day we must take steps to strengthen the gift of faith given us. Jesus suffered trials; why shouldn't we?

Our faith will save us from turning away from God, so it is good that we act in faith many times a day.

PRAYER. *Father of our Lord Jesus Christ, sustain us in our joy as we receive the Good News of forgiveness and salvation. May we understand the necessity to suffer challenges as did Your Son, Jesus.*

139

AN you drink the cup that I drink, or be baptized with the baptism with which I am baptized? —Mk 10:38

SEPT. 24

REFLECTION. Jesus' challenge to His disciples and to us is one that bears much reflection.

In order to live in the Kingdom with Jesus, we accept, as He did, His Father's Will. In so doing, we need to rejoice in daily trials, both spiritual and material.

PRAYER. *All-powerful Father, help us shoulder the burdens You allow us in this life. Keep us aware of Your presence to us that we might walk in the assurance of doing Your Will.*

 HEREFORE, I tell you: her many sins have been forgiven her because she has shown great love. But the one who has been forgiven little has little love. —Lk 7:47

SEPT. 25

REFLECTION. Jesus' critics were flabbergasted by His explanation of His allowing a public sinner to touch Him.

All of us are sinners. As we become consciously aware of God's love for us as well as His admonition not to judge one another, Jesus' highway to life opens for us.

PRAYER. *God of mercy, hear our prayers as we acknowledge our sinfulness. May we always seek to overcome sin and temptation with Your Divine help.*

REJOICED when they said to me, "Let us go to the house of the Lord." **SEPT.** —Ps 122:1 **26**

REFLECTION. What a great joy we have in our places of worship. Our faith that the living Jesus dwells in our churches can be a source of great consolation, peace, and joy.

Our visits are a privilege.

PRAYER. *Father of love, You sent Your Son to redeem us. Jesus remains with us till the end of time. May we take advantage of His Eucharistic Presence through our loving adoration.*

O to the hill country; bring wood and build the house that I may take pleasure in it and be glorified there, says the Lord. **SEPT.** —Hag 1:8 **27**

REFLECTION. We harvest the timber of virtue that the temples of our souls may be a fitting place for the Lord.

We enhance our temples with the gold and silver of charity, looking out for the poor and the marginal in our society.

PRAYER. *God of mercy and consolation, be with us each day as we strive to grow in holiness as we await Your great coming. May we always be prepared to meet You at any hour.*

IMON, are you asleep? Could you not keep watch for one hour? —Mk 14:37

REFLECTION. Like Peter's heart and mind, ours experience the ennui of the long struggle to be followers of Christ. Sometimes we need to seek the silence of a very private place.

Then we open our minds and hearts to the Lord that He might refresh us to continue the journey.

PRAYER. *God of peace and love, we come to You in the silence of our hearts. Help us to go forward with actions to send Your message to the world. May we always be ready and willing to lead others into the light.*

 NDEED, what can he give in exchange for his life? —Mk 8:37

REFLECTION. We are constantly bombarded on TV, in magazines and in newspapers with things we really need, according to the purveyors. On close examination, some of our "needs" could destroy us spiritually.

We need only, with God's help, to save our souls.

PRAYER. *All-powerful God, Your Son mounted the Cross stripped of all necessities. Help us to rid ourselves of the desire for possessions that burden us and distract us from our love for You.*

HENEVER I cry aloud to the Lord, He answers me from His holy mountain. —Ps 3:5

REFLECTION. In faith, we approach the Lord in our needs. He always hears us and responds in a way that we may not understand.

We believe that He hears us, and He answers us in His way.

PRAYER. *God of mercy and consolation, we turn to You in our perceived need. In faith, we know You answer with what is best for us. May we always accept Your decisions in our regard.*

 HY are you coming forth with swords and clubs to arrest Me, as though I were a bandit? —Mk 14:48

REFLECTION. Sometimes anger, rage, jealousy, spite or meanness enables us to attack our brothers and sisters with swords that pierce a heart or destroy a reputation. In this we attack Jesus.

As His followers we must be vigilant with our speech.

PRAYER. *Lord, our God, You ask us to use Your blessed gift of speech to spread Your Word. May we never defile this blessing with unkind or untrue words about others.*

THEY all ate and were satisfied. Then they gathered up the fragments that were left over—twelve full baskets.

—Mt 14:20

REFLECTION. We experience the generosity and compassion of Jesus for those who follow Him. Even for those who delay conversion and return to the Lord, leftovers assure fullness for all.

We announce the table is ready and filled with the Lord's goodness.

PRAYER. *Eternal Father, You have prepared for us a heavenly banquet. May we resist the temptations of this earth and seek the goodness of the next.*

FOR thus says the Lord God, they will be My people, and I will be their God.

—Ezek 14:11

REFLECTION. When we accept the spiritual responsibility for others, we are heartened to know that the Lord is with us in guiding others to Him, especially the children.

Our guidance calls for our faithful, serious, and constant concern for God's people.

PRAYER. *All-powerful and ever-living God, You call us to lead Your people through the challenges of life. May we, through prayer and sacrifice, keep the beacon of Your goodness shining brightly.*

AY I never boast of anything except the Cross of our Lord Jesus Christ, through which the world is crucified to me and I to the world.

OCT. 4

—Gal 6:14

REFLECTION. Jesus, through Paul, calls us to the reality of what life in the world should be today for His followers.

We are at cross-purposes with the world. Where the world seeks instant gratification on every level, we accept the mystery of suffering in our lives.

PRAYER. *All-powerful and unseen God, Your Son, Jesus Christ, was lifted up between heaven and earth that we might live forever. May we never accept the ways of the world.*

 T that time, Jesus said, "I thank You, Father, Lord of heaven and earth, because You have hidden these things from the wise and the learned and have revealed them to children."

OCT. 5

—Mt 11:25

REFLECTION. God's wisdom is available for all who would listen in simplicity and openness of mind and heart.

We need to approach Scripture, preaching, and Church teachings with a willingness to learn and correct in our lives what is missing.

PRAYER. *God, Light of all nations, fill Your people with Your Holy Spirit that we may be ready to hear and accept Your Word. May our acceptance be like Mary's.*

HAD heard of You by hearsay, but now I have seen You. Therefore I retract all I have said, and repent in dust and ashes.
—Job 42:5-6

OCT. 6

REFLECTION. When we receive the grace of conversion, Job's words ring true.

We are moved to simply allow God's Word to heal and lead us to further awareness of God's goodness and wisdom. His wisdom is a complete formula for life here and a guarantee of eternal life.

PRAYER. *God, our Father, You sent Your Son, Jesus, to bring us out of darkness into the light of Your Word. May we spend each day listening to and living Your Word to the best of our ability.*

 HAT do you think the owner of the vineyard will do to those tenants when he comes? —Mt 21:40

OCT. 7

REFLECTION. When we sin against the Lord, we destroy vestiges of His vineyard.

He wants to forgive us, and the question becomes, what will we do? Will we accept the forgiveness offered, or will we remain an enemy of the owner of our Father's house?

PRAYER. *God of power and mercy, grant us the grace of true contrition for our sins. Help us to see and embrace the light of Your forgiveness and consolation.*

146

THE Lord answered her: "Martha, Martha, you are anxious and upset about many things, when only one thing is necessary. Mary has chosen the better part, and it will not be taken away from her." —Lk 10:41-42

REFLECTION. Conversation with the Lord can easily be the most important part of our day. We do this by developing a keen awareness of the Lord's presence.

It will not distract from our duties, but enhance and sanctify our daily tasks.

PRAYER. *Almighty God and Father of light, may we always walk aware of Your presence with us in all that we say or do. Keep us from indifference and neglect regarding Your presence to us.*

IT WAS still unknown by sight to the Churches of Judea that are in Christ. They had only heard it said, "The one who was formerly persecuting us is now preaching the Faith that he had once tried to destroy."

—Gal 1:22-23

REFLECTION. The beauty of Paul's conversion is available to all. Our God awaits our return from sin and disbelief. He stands ready to receive us and bring us into full communion with all the Saints of the Church.

When burdened with sin and doubt, how can we resist?

PRAYER. *God of forgiveness and love, hear our prayers as we reach out to those who have hardened their hearts and refused Your love. May our love and kindness help them accept Your call to redemption.*

EVEN though the wicked may sprout like grass and all evildoers may prosper, they are doomed to eternal destruction, whereas You, O Lord, are exalted forever.

OCT.
10

—Ps 92:8-9

REFLECTION. Each day we are exposed to seemingly indifferent and bold arrogance toward our Lord. We do not share in these derogations because we love and serve Him.

We console ourselves in our destiny, namely, to be with the Most High Lord forever.

PRAYER. *All-powerful Father, as we walk through the valley of death, destruction, and sin, may we recall the goal of our journey, and remain faithful to Your love in all things.*

THEREFORE, I say to you: ask, and it will be given you; seek, and you will find; knock, and the door will be opened to you.

OCT.
11

—Lk 11:9

REFLECTION. Like Elijah, we will not find the Lord in the storm, the earthquake, or in the multitude of distractions of our time.

No, we find Him in the tiny whisper of a breeze, in a noisy silence. We seek the Lord in the silence of our hearts, waiting patiently for His whisper.

PRAYER. *Lord God, trusting in Your promise to be with us until the end, give us the calming patience to stand in waiting for Your call. Keep us faithful servants as You are abiding Lord.*

ESUS replied, "Blessed, rather, are those who hear the Word of God and obey it!" —Lk 11:28

OCT. 12

REFLECTION. Mary believed and hoped in God's Word. When called to answer His Word, she said yes! The more closely we hear and live the Word of God, the more like Mary we become.

Really, we receive the living God as did Mary in living His words.

PRAYER. *Merciful Father, we praise and thank You for having given us Mary as a model for living Your Word. May we, like Mary, hold fast to Your teachings, despite trials and tribulations.*

 N this mountain He will destroy the shroud over all peoples, the sheet spread over all nations; He will destroy death forever. —Isa 25:7

OCT. 13

REFLECTION. In times of worldwide unrest and local distress that may ignite the entire world, as followers of Jesus we are assured that, through the merits of His Crucifixion and Resurrection, death has been destroyed forever.

By imitating the holiness of Jesus, we will live forever.

PRAYER. *Father, all-powerful God, we turn to You in times of international conflict. Help us to console one another with Your promise of fidelity and peace for Your people.*

HEN he said to his servants, "The wedding banquet is ready, but those who were invited were not worthy of that honor." —Mt 22:8

OCT. 14

REFLECTION. In His love and care, the Lord has prepared great riches for us. Still, we turn to the passing delights of this world.

Who or what in our time can fulfill us as does the Lord? Through prayer and sacrifice, we strive to grow closer to the Lord each day.

PRAYER. *Jesus, our Lord, You invite us to the everlasting banquet in Your Father's house. Let us never stray from our journey to be with You and the Father forever.*

───────────

 CAN do all things in Him Who strengthens me. —Phil 4:13

OCT. 15

REFLECTION. When we think of the trials that Paul experienced in serving the Lord, we embrace his formula for success.

We know that we walk with God, and no challenge to our faith is too big to be overcome, for truly the Lord is with us.

PRAYER. *Lord our God You sustain us in hope and courage as we face each day the temptations of the evil one. Let us be witnesses to Your favor by preserving virtue in our lives.*

FROM the rising of the sun to its setting the Name of the Lord is to be praised.

—Ps 113:3

REFLECTION. With every sunrise we are reminded of God's tender care for His created world.

The light of day enables God's people to live their lives in the light, enhancing the opportunity to praise the Lord and share their abundance with the poor. Every act of charity is Divine praise.

PRAYER. *We praise You, Lord, God of heaven and earth, for the life You give us each day. May we always use our minds, hearts, and bodies to further Your work on earth.*

THE Lord said to him, "You Pharisees cleanse the outside of a cup and dish, but you leave the inside full of greed and wickedness."

—Lk 11:39

REFLECTION. Through a daily examination of conscience, we cleanse ourselves of any hidden sins and faults.

We always strive to be living the way of life that Jesus wanted us to follow.

PRAYER. *God of endless ages, Father of all goodness, help us to reflect in our daily lives the goodness that shines forth in Your Saints. Keep us on the narrow path to the place that You have prepared for us.*

NCE you were darkness, but now you are light in the Lord. Live as children of light. —Eph 5:8

REFLECTION. Through the abundance of opportunities we have to receive sacramental grace, we easily hope to walk always in the light of Christ. We strive to make our lives light for others.

And, without fear, we speak our beliefs in the face of contradiction.

PRAYER. *Merciful Lord, turn to Your people and fill them with sanctifying grace. May we be beacons of light for a darkened world that it may experience Your love and forgiveness.*

E has put all things under Christ's feet and has made Him the Head of the Church, which is His Body, the fullness of Him Who fills the universe in all its parts. —Eph 1:22-23

REFLECTION. Once Jesus was raised from the dead, the Father gave Him all peoples and things in creation.

As we seek the truth, we look to the life and teachings of Jesus. In our personal lives, we strive to imitate Jesus, especially His love for all people.

PRAYER. *Jesus, our Lord, we come to You as the Source of all peace, light, goodness and truth. Help us to live as You would have us live, both here and hereafter.*

I AM the Lord, and there is no other; besides Me there is no God. —Isa 45:5

OCT. 20

REFLECTION. So many gods can easily enter into our lives. Our automotive gods, our food-chain gods, our loose-tongue gods, our greed gods, our lust gods, our anger gods and our violence gods all vie for our love.

Happily, there is only one true God and He gives life forever.

PRAYER. *Almighty God and Father of light, we praise and bless You for the benefits of Your creation. May we always be faithful to You in using Your abundance.*

HE said to the crowd, "Take care to be on your guard against all kinds of greed. Life does not depend upon an abundance of one's possessions." —Lk 12:15

OCT. 21

REFLECTION. There are many wonderful, good and beautiful things in our world for which we thank God.

Still, it is important to remember that we take only our love and charity with us as we seek to gain true and eternal happiness.

PRAYER. *Father of our Lord, Jesus Christ, may we seek only Your honor and glory as we use the talents and goods You have given us. Keep any element of greed or personal accomplishment from blinding us to the true purpose of our sojourn here.*

LESSED are those servants whom the master finds awake when he arrives. Amen, I say to you, he will fasten his belt, have them recline to eat, and proceed to wait on them himself. —Lk 12:37

REFLECTION. While it is true that a high degree of vigilance and circumspection is needed the more we become immersed in the world, the outcomes of a disciplined and virtuous life are overwhelming.

It is difficult to conceive being waited upon by the Lord in His house.

PRAYER. *God of all compassion, Father of all goodness, be with us on our journey to the eternal banquet. Help us feed one another with lives of virtue and holiness.*

 ELP, O Lord, for there are no godly left; the faithful have vanished from the human race. —Ps 12:2

REFLECTION. Every day we encounter the vestiges of a society losing its integrity and honesty.

As we build up the Body of Christ, the Church, we need to be a people of universal truth. Double-speak must be driven from our minds, hearts, and tongues.

PRAYER. *God of endless ages, Father, Your Son, Jesus Christ, about to be condemned to death, was a pillar of honesty and straightforwardness. May we always imitate His integrity in the face of even fierce opposition.*

HAT will it profit a man if he gains the whole world and forfeits his very life? —Mt 16:26

REFLECTION. We are constantly bombarded by a chorus of deceivers, explaining what is wrong with a life of integrity and honesty.

They chant the siren song of happiness and contentment rooted in "new" items and conveniences.

PRAYER. *Almighty God, Creator of the universe, You invite us to be with You forever in the security of Your embrace. May we always live in this world with a prevailing awareness of our need to leave all things when You call us.*

HO may ascend the mountain of the Lord? Who may stand in His holy place? One who has clean hands and a pure heart, who does not turn his mind to vanities or swear an oath in order to deceive.
—Ps 24:3-4

REFLECTION. We are called to walk in truth, living with one another in peace.

We control our senses for the enhancement of our communities. And in unity, we seek those things that are good for all of us.

PRAYER. *God of love and mercy, help us to live as You would have us do. May we honor Your Name by living lives of peace and purity.*

O, I tell you—but unless you repent, you will all perish as they did. —Lk 13:5

REFLECTION. Jesus' message about the Galileans is one that withstands the test of time.

We must repent of our sins, and make sorrow for sin an ongoing part of our lives. Repentance will not free us of temptations, but it will save us when the evil one would entrap us.

PRAYER. *Heavenly Father, watch over us as we walk in the way of Your Son. Grant us the vision to know true conversion and to live it with the help of the Holy Spirit.*

 OU shall not harm any widow or orphan. If ever you harm them, and they cry out to Me, I will surely heed their cry. —Ex 22:21-22

REFLECTION. In so many ways, society sets up widows and orphans for the fall.

As followers of Jesus, we need to use our talents so that they may receive God's justice. We must raise our voices and prayers in favor of persecuted children and widows.

PRAYER. *Father of love and mercy, as we seek to bring Your love and compassion to those most in need, be with us as we encounter vested interests. May we stand firm in Your Name and Word.*

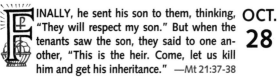

FINALLY, he sent his son to them, thinking, "They will respect my son." But when the tenants saw the son, they said to one another, "This is the heir. Come, let us kill him and get his inheritance." —Mt 21:37-38

REFLECTION. When we scheme to overcome the ways of the Lord rather than acquiring His inheritance, through sin we abandon the opportunity to be with the Lord.

Sin destroys all it touches; even the salvation offered us.

PRAYER. *Father of our Lord, Jesus Christ, You sent Your Son to us that He might show us the way to salvation. May we always listen to Him and be imitators of His love and peace.*

IT was in those days that He went onto the mountain to pray, and He spent the entire night in prayer to God. —Lk 6:12

REFLECTION. Before appointing the Twelve Apostles, Jesus went to the mountain to pray. The Apostles were to lead the Church after the Ascension.

Before every important decision in our lives, it would be of benefit to ask that God help us.

PRAYER. *Lord, our God, we turn to You in good times and bad. We praise You for being with us, especially in times of need. May we always seek Your guidance in all things.*

E said to him, "My friend, how did you gain entrance here without a wedding garment?" The man was speechless. —Mt 22:12

OCT. 30

REFLECTION. We have answered the Lord's invitation to His eternal banquet. Each day we prepare for the great event.

Our wedding garment is our life of grace and temptations overcome. We strive earnestly to persevere in good.

PRAYER. *Jesus, our Lord, at the wedding feast of Cana, You taught us parental obedience. May we always listen to the Father and accomplish His Word through Mary's intercession.*

———————

S it not written: "My house shall be called a house of prayer for all the nations"? —Mk 11:17

OCT. 31

REFLECTION. Tomorrow, as the universal Church commemorates All Saints, we see the words of Jesus fulfilled. People of every nation, time, place, background, class, age and avocation are numbered among the Saints.

We take hope, since none of us is excluded.

PRAYER. *God of endless ages, Father of all goodness, help us as we seek to follow the Saints who have gone before us. May we live their example of prayer and sacrifice.*

E Who called you is holy. Therefore, be holy yourselves in all your conduct. For Scripture says, "Be holy, for I am holy." **NOV. 1**

—1 Pet 1:15

REFLECTION. Many family, friends, and relatives who took the initiative to holiness and have gone before us give us great hope that we may someday join them in God's presence.

We ask these Saints to help us keep our minds on the great prize.

PRAYER. *Almighty God, our Father, help us to imitate our brothers and sisters who now rejoice in Your glory. May our minds and hearts be directed to keep our heavenly goal in our thoughts each day.*

F he was focusing on the splendid reward reserved for those whose death was marked by godliness, his thought was holy and devout. **NOV. 2**

—2 Mac 12:45

REFLECTION. Ever true to His promise, God has prepared a special place for those who seek to do His Will and persevere in good.

In that place, death has vanished, and pain, sickness, sorrow, anxiety, and sin are nonexistent. Only God's praise prevails.

PRAYER. *Merciful Lord, listen to our prayers for our deceased brothers and sisters. Take them from purgatory into Your perpetual light, presence, and joy.*

159

OR where your treasure is, there will your heart also be. —Mt 6:21

NOV.
3

REFLECTION. The kinds of lives we lead, spawned by our materialistic society, distract us from serious spiritual growth.

So many nonspiritual challenges, which may be legitimate, can easily cloud our vision of an eternal goal.

PRAYER. *Lord, Jesus Christ, Son of the living God, You gave Your life that we might enter heaven. In the midst of our stressed lives, keep us focused on Your love and goodness.*

 LL those who exalt themselves will be humbled, and all those who humble themselves will be exalted. —Mt 23:12

NOV.
4

REFLECTION. When we consider the fact that Jesus, the Son of God, washed the feet of His disciples, we may be more easily motivated to live in simplicity and humility.

We give way to others both on the road and in buildings, always speaking highly of others rather than ourselves.

PRAYER. *Almighty eternal God, when Your Son, Jesus, walked this earth, He did so with simplicity and humility. Help us to root out any vestiges of pride in our minds and hearts.*

ATHER, when you hold a banquet, invite the poor, the crippled, the lame, and the blind. Then indeed will you be blessed because they have no way to repay you. But you will be repaid at the resurrection of the righteous. —Lk 14:13-14

REFLECTION. Really, we throw a banquet every day. It can be just a smile, a gentle token of recognition, a simple act of courtesy for our marginalized brothers and sisters whom we meet each day.

We feed them the love and joy of Christ.

PRAYER. *Almighty God, Father of light, grant us the grace to be light, peace, and joy for others, especially the rejected of our uncompromising age.*

 O not be filled with selfish ambition or vanity, but humbly regard others as better than yourselves. —Phil 2:3

REFLECTION. Jesus shows us how to live. He cared for the sick, dined with sinners, stood silent before His accusers, traveled with the ordinary, was concerned for the welfare of His listeners, and, as Son of God, reminded us it was not for Him to select places with the Father.

What a way to live!

PRAYER. *Lord, our God. give us the courage to follow Your way, to live as You did and come to the knowledge and practice that everything we have has been given us. May our lives reflect Yours.*

N the same way, anyone of you who does not renounce all of his possessions cannot be My disciple. —Lk 14:33

REFLECTION. We have been blessed by God with many resources. Through our God-given intelligence, we have built a high standard of living.

Still, we know that we take with us only our love for one another, and charity for the poor.

PRAYER. *Lord of mercy, grant us the grace to use Your blessings for the benefit of those most in need. May we share Your gifts as generously as You give Your blessings.*

 HOEVER does not carry his own cross and follow Me cannot be My disciple. —Lk 14:27

REFLECTION. Each of us has many and varied crosses.

Jesus exhorts us to accept difficulties that come our way and use them to come closer to Him, while, at the same time, assuring our salvation. It is important to bring our minds and wills into line with Jesus'.

PRAYER. *Father in heaven, Creator of all, Your Son, Jesus Christ, came to save us for the Kingdom. He calls us to follow Your Will as He did. May we always be open to Your words and commands.*

WHICH one of you, if you have a hundred sheep and lose one of them, will not leave the ninety-nine in the wilderness and go after the one that is lost until he finds it? —Lk 15:4

REFLECTION. Jesus asks us never to give up on anyone, especially the young, if they seem lost.

We go after them so that we might lift them up and bring them back to the fold to share the life of Christ with their brothers and sisters.

PRAYER. *God, Light of nations, Good Shepherd of the universe, we are privileged to be Your helpers in healing those You came to cure. May we never cease assisting them with our prayers and charity.*

HAVE you not read this Scripture: "The stone that the builders rejected has become the cornerstone; by the Lord this has been done, and it is wonderful in our eyes"? —Mk 12:10-11

REFLECTION. As we grow closer to the Lord, we come to realize more and more how the sustaining factor in our lives and in the progress of the Church is Jesus Christ.

He is our foundation, and we depend on Him to keep us from falling into the pit!

PRAYER. *All-powerful God, You gave us Your Son, Jesus Christ, to sustain us in the battle against evil. May we always build our spiritual house on the solid foundation of Your Word.*

UNBELIEVING generation, how much longer shall I remain with you? How much longer must I put up with you? —Mk 9:19

REFLECTION. While we may live in an age of unbelief, and a society that proclaims, "challenge authority," we focus on deepening our faith.

In humility and joy, we reach out to those in need; we abandon the hunt for riches and instant gratification.

PRAYER. *God of mercy, as we strive to live Your Word, forgive our shortcomings, consider our goodwill and strengthen us in faith that we might complete the race.*

 OR the grace of God has appeared, bringing salvation to the entire human race. It teaches us to reject godless ways and worldly desires, and in the present age to lead lives that are temperate, just, and godly. —Tit 2:11-12

REFLECTION. Paul's letter to Titus echoes Jesus' assurance that God's grace is sufficient for us, no matter our condition.

This gives us hope in times of temptation, disappointment, and scandal. We do not lose hope since we believe that we are filled with the Lord's love and grace.

PRAYER. *Eternal Father, may we always reject all that is not of Your doing, creation, and Kingdom. Help us to live in Your grace till You send Your Angel to take us to the place prepared for us.*

SINCE my conduct has been just and upright, do not abandon me to those who oppress me. Guarantee the well-being of Your servant; do not allow the arrogant to oppress me. —Ps 119:121-122

NOV. 13

REFLECTION. Each day, as we offer our prayers, works, and joys of the day to the Lord, we realize that right living will help us win the crown.

With humility, charity, and peaceful hearts, we walk the narrow way of Christian goodness.

PRAYER. *Father of light, it is our joy to live in the brilliance of Your presence. May we always stay out of the shadows of death and destruction.*

ONE of them, when he realized that he had been cured, came back, praising God in a loud voice. He prostrated himself at the feet of Jesus and thanked Him. —Lk 17:15-16

NOV. 14

REFLECTION. As a people, Church, and nation, we have been blessed in so many special ways, both individually and as a community. Ours should be a culture of thanksgiving.

We acknowledge daily our awareness of how abundantly God's grace engulfs us. We let our lives reflect this.

PRAYER. *God, our Father, Source of all goodness and blessings, we offer grateful praise and thanksgiving for Your generosity in our regard. May we imitate Your abundance in the way that we share our gifts with others.*

ND this is love: when we walk according to His Commandments. This is the Commandment that you have heard from the beginning, and you must follow it. —2 Jn 6

NOV.
15

REFLECTION. While we strive each day to observe all God's Commandments, we concentrate on the greatest Commandment, that we love one another.

Of necessity, the observance of the great Commandment guarantees the fulfillment of all.

PRAYER. *God of love and mercy, be with us as we seek to accomplish Your will in this world. May we turn to You in times of need. Help us to love all without exception.*

ILL not God, therefore, grant justice to His elect who cry out to Him day and night? Will He delay in answering their pleas?

—Lk 18:7

NOV.
16

REFLECTION. Once we are baptized, we are God's chosen ones. We need but call out to Him, especially in times of temptation.

He will always hear us, and His answer will be swift and sure. We have nothing to fear when we walk with God.

PRAYER. *All-powerful Father, Your children look to You in times of temptation. Keep us free of sin that we might be worthy to live with You forever.*

HE future bodes well for him who is generous in helping those in need and who conducts his affairs with justice. He will never be swayed; the righteous man will be remembered forever.

NOV. 17

—Ps 112:5-6

REFLECTION. In the workaday world, where giving and taking orders is commonplace, we remember those individuals who treat us fairly.

God wants us to be fair with one another, seeking justice on all occasions.

PRAYER. *God of peace and justice, we follow Your Son, Jesus, in bringing peace and justice to our communities. May we always stand fast in Your truth, protecting the innocent and needy.* _____

 HARM is deceitful and beauty empty; but a woman who fears the Lord is to be praised.

NOV. 18

—Prov 31:30

REFLECTION. In every age and every time, women have loved the Lord and formed the foundation of society. We look to the Theresas, Catherine of Siena, Elizabeth Ann Seton and our Blessed Mother, to mention only a few.

We strive to imitate their great love for God.

PRAYER. *Father in heaven, Creator of all, Your holy Church has raised men and women of every age to the altar of sanctity. May we never fail to imitate the virtues of our Saints.*

OW countless are Your works, O Lord; by Your wisdom You have made them all; the earth abounds with Your creatures. —Ps 104:24

NOV. 19

REFLECTION. We celebrate all the good things of the earth. We consider it a blessing to live among peoples who have been created in the image and likeness of God, filled with the Holy Spirit.

We respect one another in the Lord.

PRAYER. *Almighty Father, grant us the fullness of Your Spirit that we may realize Your goodness manifest in all our brothers and sisters. May we always respect one another as Your Son respected us.*

 E shouted, "Jesus, Son of David, have pity on me!" —Lk 18:38

NOV. 20

REFLECTION. As sinners, we are blind to God's great love for us. We are beggars seeking forgiveness. We simply shout to Jesus to save us from ourselves.

We step out by forgiving one another.

PRAYER. *God of mercy and consolation, hear us as we cry out for forgiveness of our sins. We turn back to You, returning to Your house to be embraced like the prodigals we are.*

THEN He entered the temple and began to drive out those who were engaging in selling, saying to them, "It is written, 'My house shall be a house of prayer,' but you have made it a den of thieves." **NOV. 21**

—Lk 19:45-46

REFLECTION. As temples of the Lord, we can easily call Jesus' anger upon us by becoming attached to material things.

We seek the Lord in all things. We praise the Lord for the beauty and wisdom of His creation. Still, we strive to remain detached from objects.

PRAYER. *God of endless ages, Father, help us to see the wisdom of Your creation and reflect on the beauty of Your presence among us. May we always seek to live detached from the worldly and live only for the eternal.*

ONE of the elders said to me, "Do not weep. The Lion of the tribe of Judah, the Root of David, has triumphed, and thus has won the right to open the scroll and its seven seals." **NOV. 22**

—Rev 5:5

REFLECTION. The ancestry of the resurrected Jesus clearly defines His role in our salvation. In light of the Resurrection miracle, our hope soars and our confidence deepens.

What more assurance do we need to grow in the love of God?

PRAYER. *God of all compassion, Father of all goodness, we rejoice in the knowledge and love of our resurrected Christ. Our destiny has been assured, a place prepared. May we respond generously to Your invitation to holiness.*

ET all mankind be silent in the presence of the Lord! For He stirs forth from His holy dwelling. —Zec 2:17

NOV.
23

REFLECTION. One of the blessings of our age is the opportunity for moments of silence.

Once silence is achieved, the presence of the Lord blossoms into a fullness of delight and refreshment.

PRAYER. *Father of our Lord, Jesus Christ, Your Son taught us how to pray. We seek a refreshing place alone or accept a bed of pain in silence. May we always rest in Your presence.*

 VERY day He was teaching in the temple. But the chief priests, the scribes, and the leaders of the people plotted to kill Him. —Lk 19:47

NOV.
24

REFLECTION. In living lives of goodness, we teach the ways of the Lord.

Many who do not accept Christ's teachings, in a variety of subtle ways, seek to destroy our virtue and foster the death of sin in us.

PRAYER. *Lord, our God, watch over us as the forces of evil seek to destroy our relationship with You. May we walk in Your light with courage and grace.*

N Christ and through His Blood we have re- **NOV.** demption and the forgiveness of our sins. In **25** accord with the riches of His grace, God lavished on us all wisdom and insight.

—Eph 1:7-8

REFLECTION. Christ shed His Blood on the Cross that we might live forever. Through His redeeming Blood, like an endless river flowing from Mount Calvary, Christ beckons us to be blood of His Blood, flesh of His flesh that we might be light now and forever.

Dare we hesitate?

PRAYER. *God of mercy, through Your great love for Your people, You saved us through Jesus' bloody sacrifice. May we be willing to suffer our daily crosses with Jesus that they may bring us to salvation.*

 HO is this that comes forth like the **NOV.** dawn, fair as the moon, bright as **26** the sun, formidable as an army with banners? —Song 6:10

REFLECTION. The blessed child of Joachim and Anne gave the world its brightest hope of eternal salvation. Born into the obscurity of poverty and marginality, Mary's birth guaranteed Incarnation and redemption.

All generations call her Blessed.

PRAYER. *Lord, Jesus Christ, Son of the living God, Your mother's birth reflected the circumstances of Your coming to earth. May we imitate Mary's poverty, detachment, and humility that we might bring souls to You.*

OREVER rejoice in what I create; for I create Jerusalem as a joy and its people as a delight. —Isa 65:18

REFLECTION. The prophets of old longed for life with a forgiving God. God's place was envisioned as a place of joy for all His people. And God would share their delight in His presence among them.

We avoid sin as we seek the New Jerusalem.

PRAYER. *Almighty and ever-loving God, You fulfill the promise of Jesus to prepare a place for us. Help us to live Your Word completely as we prepare to joyfully enter the new and eternal Jerusalem.*

 HIS is the name by which the city will be called: The Lord Our Righteousness. —Jer 33:16

REFLECTION. We know and believe that the Messiah has come into our lives and our world.

Recalling the events of over 2000 years ago provides an excellent opportunity to study how we as individuals are impacted by Christ's coming to earth.

PRAYER. *Lord, our God, be with us as we come into new beginnings. Bless our prayers, virtuous strivings, and charitable outreach as we ache to be worthy of the Messiah.*

N those days and at that time I will cause a righteous branch to spring up from the line of David; He will do what is just and upright in the land. —Jer 33:15

NOV. 29

REFLECTION. Our ancestors longed for a fair and equitable justice in their land. Their hope was in the Messiah of the family of David.

Jesus is our justice, which we are called to uphold with everyone.

PRAYER. *God of love, we praise and thank You for having given us true justice in our day through the ministry of Jesus. Help us to imitate His justice.*

 AY the Lord cause your love to increase and overflow for one another and for everyone else, just as our love does for you. —1 Thes 3:12

NOV. 30

REFLECTION. Our love for one another can be embraced as a part of our reminder how the Child Jesus accepted the difficulties of humanity when He was born for our salvation.

He asks nothing more than our love for one another.

PRAYER. *God of love and mercy, look down upon Your people as we strive to imitate the great love that Jesus had for us in walking with us on this earth. May we always love one another, without exception, as Jesus loved us.*

173

HERE will be signs in the sun, the moon, and the stars. . . . —Lk 21:25

DEC. 1

REFLECTION. We Christians have great expectations, and with anticipatory joy we look forward to Christ's Second Coming.

We remind ourselves to ready our minds, hearts, and spirits for the moment of the Messiah Christ's coming.

PRAYER. *Heavenly Father, we bend our spirit to Your Will so that having walked in the justice of Your Word, we may embrace our Savior with peace and tranquility. Strengthen us in our weakness.*

 E have been told that some among you are living a life of idleness, not working but acting as busybodies. —2 Thes 3:11

DEC. 2

REFLECTION. As individuals supporting the mosaic of God's people, we serve the entire Christian Church in our personal spiritual growth.

We lighten the burden of all through personal holiness.

PRAYER. *Lord, our God, direct our minds and hearts in the way of simplicity as we walk the path to everlasting life. Help us to detach ourselves from incidentals that do not concern us.*

HEN the crowds asked him, "What then should we do?" he said to them in reply, "Anyone who has two coats must share with the person who has none. . . ." —Lk 3:10-11

DEC.
3

REFLECTION. Do we bring warmth and care to the cold stable by our own personal compassion, concern, and hope for those who have less than we?

As we prepare to go to Bethlehem, let us vest ourselves with prayer, fasting, and charity for God's poor.

PRAYER. *God, our Father, open our eyes so that we may see the reality of Your call for us to share all we have with Your poor. You bless us with this great opportunity. Grace us with Your spirit of generosity and love.*

 UT you, Bethlehem-Ephrathah, too small to be among the clans of Judah, from you shall come forth for Me One Who is to rule in Israel. . . . —Mic 5:1

DEC.
4

REFLECTION. The Holy One Who is to rule over Israel comes forth from the least of the clans of Judah.

In the midst of commerce, trade, daily grind and opulent pastimes of the rich, a poor maiden girl deprives herself of home and hearth to be with her elderly cousin, about to give birth.

PRAYER. *God, our Father, Your Son, Jesus Christ, left Your heavenly Kingdom to walk on this earth so that we might have eternal life. Grant us the wisdom to walk with the Lord in all things, especially a spirit of detachment.*

ND then they will see the Son of Man coming in a cloud with power and great glory. —Lk 21:27

REFLECTION. In this great time of anticipation, we open ourselves up to the Second Coming of Jesus. He will come with power and glory that will accomplish our salvation.

We live so as not to deprive ourselves of this goal.

PRAYER. *Almighty God of power and glory, You sent Your Son to invite us to the heavenly banquet. As we prepare to receive Him again, help us to ready ourselves for eternal life.*

 LL mankind shall see the salvation of God. —Lk 3:6

REFLECTION. In our very prayer, we spread the Good News of salvation, while, at the same time, echo John the Baptist's baptism of repentance and conversion.

All humankind will hear and heed God's Word.

PRAYER. *Heavenly Father, we take heart in the Good News of the Messiah. Help us to tend and mend our lives that we may become beacons of salvation for all who want to live with Your people in Your light.*

E vigilant at all times, praying for the strength to survive all those things that will take place and to stand in the presence of the Son of Man. —Lk 21:36

DEC. 7

REFLECTION. Every day we are subject to the temptations of the evil one.

Through the power of prayer we stand fast in our resolution to follow Jesus closely.

PRAYER. *God, our Father, we know our personal weakness, and we pray for the grace to stand firm in the Lord. May this day be one of victory over temptation and death.*

 EMOVE your robe of mourning and affliction, O Jerusalem, and adorn yourself forever with the splendor of the glory of God. —Bar 5:1

DEC. 8

REFLECTION. Each day, as we live according to God's Will in our regard, we clothe ourselves with the wisdom and love of God.

We vest ourselves with the joy of knowing our Redeemer is near at hand.

PRAYER. *Loving Father, help Your people to be aware of Your great love for us. Keep us in Your good graces, and let us walk always in the light of Christ.*

AND for this I pray: that your love may increase ever more and more in knowledge and full insight to enable you to discover what is really important, so that on the Day of Christ you may be pure and blameless.

DEC.
9

—Phil 1:9-10

REFLECTION. Like the early Christians of Paul's Church, we pray for one another that we may be worthy of the Redeemer when He comes.

We purify our hearts of all that could bring us into the ruin of sin.

PRAYER. *God, our Father, we earnestly beg You to keep us in Your grace. Let not the wiles of the devil bring us to a tragic end.*

HE journeyed throughout the entire region of the Jordan valley, proclaiming a baptism of repentance for the forgiveness of sins. —Lk 3:3

DEC.
10

REFLECTION. The Word of God speaks to us plainly as John the Baptist spoke to those who went out into the desert to see him.

We know honestly that repentance is the foundation for the forgiveness of sin.

PRAYER. *God, our Father, we turn to You in our need. Forgive us our sins that we may be ready for the coming of Your Son.*

HE kindly man will be blessed, for he shares his bread with the poor.

—Prov 22:9

DEC. 11

REFLECTION. In freedom, we dwell in a land of plenty. All the more reason we need to resolve to share in a very generous way with the poor.

What we give to the poorest, we give to Christ.

PRAYER. *God, our Father, You allowed Your Son to be born into poverty and be raised up in poverty. Open our eyes to this message so that we might save ourselves through sharing the many blessings You give us.*

 N that day it will be said to Jerusalem: Have no fear, O Zion, do not let your hands grow weak. The Lord, your God, is in your midst, a mighty Savior. . . . —Zep 3:16-17

DEC. 12

REFLECTION. The words of Zephaniah parallel our inner thoughts as we go about our daily tasks in great anticipation of the presence of the saving Lord in our minds and hearts, as well as among His people.

We live this very anticipation in the peace of the accomplished Incarnation.

PRAYER. *God, our Father, You sent Your Son to save us from our sins. Take from us those fears generated by worldliness, and enable us to live in the peace of the Christ Child.*

ET your kindness be known to everyone. The Lord is near. —Phil 4:5

DEC.
13

REFLECTION. As the day of our Lord's birth grows closer, we cover ourselves in the mantle of kindness.

We imitate the virtues of the Child-God, so gentle, forgiving, and kind.

PRAYER. *God of love, mercy, and compassion, hear the voices of Your people as we aspire to the kindness and gentleness of Jesus.*

 ND with many other exhortations, he proclaimed the Good News to the people. —Lk 3:18

DEC.
14

REFLECTION. In our everyday lives, we receive many signs of the Good News being put into practice.

People are kind to one another; the elderly are cared for; the sick-poor are housed, all in the Name of the Lord.

PRAYER. *God, our Father, You reached out to Your people in their great need for salvation. Help us to meet the needs of those less fortunate than we.*

AND it was by this "will" that we have been consecrated through the offering of the body of Jesus Christ once for all. —Heb 10:10

DEC. 15

REFLECTION. From the very outset of His life, Jesus offered His body for our souls. He experienced cold and poverty on the day of His birth. As a Babe, He had to flee with His parents for His life.

Our personal sacrifices are a response to His coming for us.

PRAYER. *God, our Father, You enable us to live in the freedom of Your children. In imitation of Jesus, help us to chasten our bodies as a sacrifice for the good of many.*

 IN those days, Mary set out and journeyed in haste into the hill country to a town of Judah where she entered the house of Zechariah and greeted Elizabeth. —Lk 1:39-40

DEC. 16

REFLECTION. On a mission of love and mercy, Mary went to help her older cousin, Elizabeth, who was pregnant. Mary anticipated her cousin's needs in time of stress.

As mother of Jesus, Mary is a model for those who seek to help others in times of need.

PRAYER. *God, our Father, in choosing Mary, You have given us an example of great charity. Help us to imitate Mary so that we might bring Your love and mercy to others.*

LESSED is she who believed that what the Lord has said to her will be fulfilled. —Lk 1:45

DEC. 17

REFLECTION. Elizabeth praised Mary for her great faith.

Her words reflect our faith, encouraging us to ever deepen our faith so as to be ready to greet God's Messenger.

PRAYER. *Almighty Father, You have conferred on us the great gift of Faith. Help us to live our Faith in imitation of Mary and the Saints.*

———————

HY, O Lord, do you let us stray from Your ways and harden our hearts so that we do not fear You? —Isa 63:17

DEC. 18

REFLECTION. So many times we wish that we were incapable of falling into sin.

Often we challenge ourselves for being so stubborn and hardhearted, particularly when it comes to God's message and His messengers.

PRAYER. *O Lord, my God, we ask You to save us from ourselves. Take away any hardness of heart that may lead us into sin.*

YET, O Lord, You are our Father; we are the clay, You the potter; we are all the work of Your hand. —Isa 64:7

DEC. 19

REFLECTION. The realization that our very existence is the result of the working hand of God leads us to the knowledge that we walk always in the presence of God.

And we know full well that we have been redeemed.

PRAYER. *Loving Father, we love and praise You for Your great goodness in having created us to be with You. Guard our ways that we might reach our home with Mary and the Saints forever.*

———————

HE will keep you steadfast until the very end, so that you may be blameless on the Day of our Lord Jesus Christ. —1 Cor 1:8

DEC. 20

REFLECTION. As we look forward to the birth of Jesus, we rejoice in the redemptive graces that come to us in His birth.

We feel security in the knowledge of Jesus' mission to those who love Him.

PRAYER. *O Lord, be with us in the joys of looking forward to being sustained by Your goodness. Make our wills Your own so that we may walk in the freedom of the sisters and brothers of Jesus.*

KEEP watch . . . lest he arrive unexpectedly and find you asleep. What I say to you, I say to all: Keep awake!

—Mk 13:35-37

REFLECTION. The birth of Jesus will bring a new order to the people of God.

Saved from our sins, we need only watch for the coming of the Lord with lives lived in accordance with His Will.

PRAYER. *God, our Father, in this great preparation time, may we resolve to seek only the good You ask of us in the example of Jesus, Your Son.*

THEREFORE the Lord Himself will give you a sign. The virgin is with child and shall bear a Son, and shall name Him Immanuel.

—Isa 7:14

REFLECTION. The words of the prophet Isaiah heighten our sense of expectation of the Messiah's coming. We can only imagine how those who lived immediately before Christ's birth felt. Many were anxious to believe; others perhaps were indifferent.

Where do we stand today?

PRAYER. *God, our Father, help us to cleanse our minds and hearts so that we may be worthy to receive the Messiah Who is soon to be with us.*

OSEPH, son of David, do not be afraid to receive Mary into your home as your wife. For this Child has been conceived in her womb through the Holy Spirit. —Mt 1:20

DEC. 23

REFLECTION. Joseph's role in the birth of Jesus is rooted in his deep sense of faith and obedience to God's messengers.

Like Joseph, we are called to bolster our faith, using every means given us through God's Word.

PRAYER. *God, our Father, we give You thanks and praise for the good example of Joseph in accepting his role in our redemption. May we imitate his closeness to Jesus all our days.*

 ROM this man's descendants, God has fulfilled His promise by raising up for Israel a Savior, Jesus. —Acts 13:23

DEC. 24

REFLECTION. The great goodness of God toward His people calls us to a greater love for the Father.

His Son will come to us in the morrow so that we might live in the light forever.

PRAYER. *God, our Father, with hearts full of expectation, Your sons and daughters turn to You in gratitude in this great moment of anticipatory joy.*

HE people who walked in darkness have seen a great light; on those who lived in a land of darkness a light has shone.

DEC. 25

—Isa 9:1

REFLECTION. Our winter of sin and coldness of heart is warmed with the brilliance of the newborn King. Songs of heavenly choirs fill the air as well as our minds and hearts.

The promise has been fulfilled, and we praise God with great joy.

PRAYER. *Lord, our God, we pray for the wisdom to go to Bethlehem and adore the newborn Child. Grant us the grace to always walk in His light.*

N Angel of the Lord appeared to them, and the glory of the Lord shone around them. They were terror-stricken.

DEC. 26

—Lk 2:9

REFLECTION. Roused from their sleep with heavenly music and great light, the shepherds at first feared for their lives. Instantly, they knew their lives were safe forever in the birth of Jesus.

We share that security in Jesus.

PRAYER. *God, our Father, as we await the heavenly messenger, may we take to heart the Christmas message given the shepherds by Your Angels. May we respond with similar faith.*

THEN the other disciple who had reached the tomb first also went inside, and he saw and believed.

—Jn 20:8

DEC. 27

REFLECTION. John, Apostle and Evangelist, writes of what he saw, namely the evidence of Jesus' Resurrection from the dead.

The birth, death, and Resurrection of Jesus lead us to walk with joy and care on the road to eternal life.

PRAYER. *Lord, our God, may we always rejoice in the birth of Jesus by living as Resurrection people, destined to be with the raised Christ forever.*

OUR help is in the Name of the Lord, the Maker of heaven and earth.

—Ps 124:8

DEC. 28

REFLECTION. The horror of the slaughter of innocent children challenges our faith.

But we know that the Creator of heaven and earth is with us, sustaining our faith and destiny.

PRAYER. *Heavenly Father, Your Son came into the world as a Child. May we, like Him, care for the children of the world, especially those who are abandoned.*

ING to the Lord and bless His Name; proclaim His salvation day after day.

—Ps 96:2

DEC. 29

REFLECTION. Someone once said, "A good laugh is sunshine in the house."

We should be all smiles in the house of the Lord, rejoicing in the birth of the Christ Child, raising our minds and voices in prayerful praise.

PRAYER. *God, our Father, You created us in Your image and likeness. May we fill our hearts with the joyful praise that is a constant reminder of Your Kingdom.*

 E got up, and took the Child and His mother, and departed that night for Egypt.

—Mt 2:14

DEC. 30

REFLECTION. Father, mother, and Child flee danger.

Parents take responsibility for their children in a great covenant with the Lord. Families find holiness in love, care, and concern for one another.

PRAYER. *Almighty God, Your plan of creation rests on the bedrock of family. May we always love and support our families.*

OWEVER, to those who did accept Him and who believed in His Name He granted the power to become children of God. —Jn 1:12

REFLECTION. Our lives are enhanced through our faith in the birth of Jesus.

They are further enhanced in our knowledge that we are indeed the children of God.

PRAYER. *God, our Father, make us like Your Son, Jesus, always faithful to Your Will.*

———————

PRAYERS OF INSPIRATION

Prayer for the Zest for Living

HEAVENLY Father,
no matter what may befall me,
let me never lose my zest for life
or my appreciation of this beautiful world
that You have created and made available to
    me.
Keep ever before my eyes the glory of being
    alive,
the wondrous freshness of each new day,
and the magnificence of the creatures
    around us
as they sing Your praises by their very being.

Do not let me focus on my own troubles
and remain blind to life's wonders.
Teach me how to take time each day
to thank You for all Your gifts to us,
singing Your glory with all Your creatures
in union with Your Son Jesus Christ.

Prayer to Walk with God

LORD,
the life of today is frantic and delirious.
I often find myself lost in the crowd,
conditioned by whatever surrounds me,
unable to stop and reflect.

Make me rediscover
and live

the value of walking toward You,
laden and compromised
with all the reality
of today's world;
the consciousness of feeling
constantly called by name, by You;
the grace of responding freely,
of taking Your Word
as light
to all my steps.

Prayer to Discern God's Plan
Made Known in Everyday Life

LORD Jesus Christ,
You came to earth and had an immeasurable effect
on the lives of those whom You met.
Let me realize that Your Father works
through people I meet every day of my life.
In every encounter and in every event,
You are coming to meet me—
if only I can discern Your presence.
And by my own life I also become for others
a bearer of God's plan.
Help me to respond to Your call gladly
when it comes to me each day in others.

Prayer to Be Truly Human

LORD Jesus Christ,
You came to earth and embraced our
humanity,

thereby teaching us how to be truly human.
Help me to follow Your example
and so bring out in myself all that is fully
    human.
Teach me to appreciate the immense good
that lies in being human,
climaxed by the gift of genuine self-giving.

Enable me to make use of all Your gifts
in accord with the purpose for which You
    gave them
and for the good of others.
Make me realize that only when I am gen-
    uinely human
can I be a true follower of You.

Prayer for Love of God

MY GOD and Father,
I believe that You are Love itself.
Give me a deeper love for You.
I believe that You sent Your Son Jesus
to save the world
and that Your enduring love is always
at work among us.

Help me to keep Your Commandments,
for only then do I truly love You.
Give me a love for You that drives out fear,
a love worthy of a child of God.
Through love may I be incorporated into
    Jesus Christ,
Your Son, the true God and eternal Life!

OTHER OUTSTANDING BOOKS IN THIS SERIES

BIBLE DAY BY DAY—By Rev. John C. Kersten, S.V.D. Minute Bible meditations for every day, including a short Scripture text and brief reflection. Printed in two colors with 300 illustrations.　　　　**No. 150**

MINUTE MEDITATIONS FROM THE POPES—By Rev. Jude Winkler, OFM Conv. Minute meditations for every day of the year, using the words of twentieth-century Popes. Printed and illustrated in two colors.　　　　**No. 175**

AUGUSTINE DAY BY DAY—By Rev. John E. Rotelle, O.S.A. Minute meditations for every day of the year, taken from the writings of Augustine, with a concluding prayer also from the Saint.　　　　**No. 170**

DAILY MEDITATIONS WITH AUGUSTINE—By Rev. John E. Rotelle, O.S.A. Companion to the best-selling *Augustine Day by Day,* this book provides meditations and prayers for every day, taken from the writings of Saint Augustine. Printed in two colors. 192 pages.　　　　**No. 176**

WORDS OF COMFORT FOR EVERY DAY—By Rev. Joseph T. Sullivan. Short meditation for every day, including a Scripture text and a meditative prayer to God the Father. Printed in two colors. 192 pages.　　　　**No. 186**

LIVING WISDOM FOR EVERY DAY—By Rev. Bennet Kelley, C.P. Choice texts from St. Paul of the Cross, one of the true masters of spirituality, and a prayer for each day.　　　　**No. 182**

MINUTE MEDITATIONS FOR EACH DAY—By Rev. Bede Naegele, O.C.D. This very attractive book offers a short Scripture text, a practical reflection, and a meaningful prayer for each day of the year.　　　　**No. 190**

EVERY DAY IS A GIFT—Introduction by Rev. Frederick Schroeder. Popular meditations for every day, featuring a text from Sacred Scripture, a quotation from the writings of a Saint, and a meaningful prayer. Includes ribbon marker.　　　　**No. 195**

GIANT TYPE EDITION—This popular book offered in larger, easy-to-read print.　　　　**No. 196**

DAILY MEDITATIONS WITH THE HOLY SPIRIT—By Rev. Jude Winkler, OFM Conv. Contains a Scripture reading, a reflection, and a prayer for every day of the year. Fr. Winkler offers us an opportunity to develop a closer relationship with the Holy Spirit and apply the fruits of our meditation to our everyday lives.　　　　**No. 198**

www.catholicbookpublishing.com

ISBN 978-1-937913-55-7

90000